Better Homes and Gardens®

Celebrate

Volume 1

table *of* contents

let the year begin

page 6 Usher in the new year with clever decorating ideas and celebratory salutes to start off the year in style. From ways to refresh your living space to smile-inducing gifts, this chapter invites you to look forward with grand anticipation.

welcome spring

page 32 As the weather turns warmer, focus on bright new beginnings. Enjoy inspiring ideas that boost your creativity for unforgettable get-togethers, spectacular decorations, best-ever gift giving, and so much more.

savor the seasons

page 60 Serve delectable foods that make every meal something to celebrate. From yummy breakfast recipes to the best desserts imaginable, these kitchen-tested recipes will find their way onto your favorites list in no time.

salute summer

page 96 There's something about summer that makes everything brighter. Let tranquility and happiness flow with feel-good decorating approaches and party themes that make the most of the warm-weather season.

boo-tify your home

page 122 Brew up a little Halloween magic for your family and friends this year. Fiendish trims, unexpected accents, and tasty treats are yours if you dare. These creative concoctions will please every ghoul and goblin.

easy does it

Make wonderful projects and delicious recipes that take little time, yet warrant big applause.

- do me a favor page 30
- may day surprises page 58
- garden-fresh fix-ups page 94
- school rules page 120
- not-so-tricky treats page 152

patterns *pages 154–158* • index *pages 159–160*

Better Homes and Gardens.

Celebrate

MEREDITH CONSUMER MARKETING
Vice President, Consumer Marketing: David Ball
Consumer Product Marketing Director: Steve Swanson
Consumer Product Marketing Manager: Wendy Merical
Business Manager: Ron Clingman
Associate Director, Production: Al Rodruck

WATERBURY PUBLICATIONS, INC.
Contributing Editors: Sue Banker, Lois White
Contributing Art Director: Cathy Brett
Editorial Director: Lisa Kingsley
Associate Editor: Tricia Laning
Creative Director: Ken Carlson
Associate Design Director: Doug Samuelson
Contributing Copy Editor: Terri Fredrickson
Contributing Proofreaders: Gretchen Kauffman, Peg Smith

BETTER HOMES AND GARDENS® MAGAZINE
Editor in Chief: Gayle Goodson Butler
Art Director: Michael D. Belknap
Deputy Editor, Food and Entertaining: Nancy Wall Hopkins
Senior Food Editor: Richard Swearinger
Associate Food Editor: Erin Simpson
Editorial Assistant: Renee Irey

President: Tom Harty
Executive Vice President: Andy Sareyan
Vice President, Production: Bruce Heston

MEREDITH CORPORATION
Chairman and Chief Executive Officer: Stephen M. Lacy

In Memoriam: E.T. Meredith III (1933–2003)

Pura Vida

Last summer I was fortunate to travel to Costa Rica in celebration of a friend's landmark birthday. That spectacular vacation reminded me of how "the little things" can transform an ordinary moment or day into the extraordinary.

For example, every morning the resort dressed the tables with a new twist. It was a small fresh floral centerpiece one day and bright color place mats the next. Those little touches added to the atmosphere, starting our day with joy.

And the foods! They were delicious and the presentations unforgettable. While sometimes the "aha" was as simple as fruit cut into artistic shapes, these extras transformed mealtimes into special events.

When it was time to depart, we wanted to thank our wonderful housekeeping staff with more than a simple "thank you." So on the desk in our room we arranged a handful of seashells into a flower shape, rolling our leftover foreign bills as the stems. We also left a note that said "Pura Vida." Depending on whom you talk to in Costa Rica, this widely used phrase can mean anything from "full of life" to "thank you."

It's our hope that this first edition of *Celebrate* inspires you to make every day extraordinary. This brand-new *Better Homes and Gardens*® book focuses on the months that precede the year-end holiday season (for that, we offer *Celebrate the Season*).

You don't need to wait until the Christmas season to indulge in decadent recipes. Treat your friends and family to something spectacular today. Be inspired by the fresh takes on spring and summer decorating. Craft a gift or throw a party that beams with thoughtfulness. Discover Halloween tricks and treats that will be remembered for many hauntings to come.

So whether it's a springtime holiday or an autumn football game, you can count on *Celebrate* to help you make the very most of it.

Pura Vida!

Sue Banker

let the YEAR BEGIN

Start off the new year right with fresh ideas for your home and family. From crafting decorations to celebrating winter's-end holidays, this chapter honors the beginning of the new calendar year with style.

Cabin Fever

Once the Christmas decorations are put away, look at your home as a blank canvas. Instead of heading back to your usual preholiday decor, start out the year by enlivening your space with souvenirs that allow you to relive vacations past.

Knock on Wood

■ A roll of faux-wood shelf liner and a set of inexpensive plastic place mats join forces to anchor this place setting. Trace the place mat outline on the back of the adhesive shelf liner, cut out, and adhere. Tie rolled napkins with leather cord and add a souvenir charm or pennant to finish the look.

Scene Setting

Transform your dining room into a rustic getaway. Cover the table with a rugged camp blanket and toss blooms into an enamelware pitcher.

Message in a Bottle

Turn a postcard or photograph into a memorable time capsule. Place the picture card in a jar, add a few natural elements collected from a trip, and tie a length of leather cord around the jar's neck.

Armchair Traveler

■ Keep vacation memories in mind with a photo-turned-pillow. With an ink-jet printer, print a photo onto special paper-backed fabric and use it as the centerpiece for a handmade pillow or readymade pillow cover.

Out in the Open

■ To create a three-dimensional scrapbook, arrange vacation mementos on a tray where you'll see them every day. Line the tray with a souvenir map and protect it with a piece of glass or acrylic.

What A Dish

Fine China

■ Show off family photos and a collection of decorative plates all together with this easy afternoon project. For an eclectic look, choose plates or serving dishes in a variety of sizes and with different rims. For a more unified appearance, choose dishes from the same pattern in several sizes.

What You'll Need...

- ☐ enlarged photo printouts on cardstock or adhesive-back paper
- ☐ compass with pencil
- ☐ double-stick tape (optional)
- ☐ plates and/or serving dishes

1 Print photos large enough to fit the plate center, using adhesive-back paper (if desired).

2 With a compass set to half the diameter of the plate center, trace a circle on the back of the image; cut out.

3 Adhere the photo to the plate, using double-stick tape (if needed).

It's the perfect time of year to catch up on photo organization. Spend time sorting, then serve your favorite photographs in frames fashioned from everyday items such as plates and hand mirrors.

Love Notes

Make someone's Valentine's Day with a gift
that's crafted by hand and comes from the heart.

Sweet Nothings

■ Tuck a small homemade card into a bouquet or a loved one's lunch bag. Heart-shape paper punches and rubber stamps make mass production easy.

Pretty in Pink

■ Romance is in the air and on the table with this easy but elegant setting. Decorate a heart-shape box with pink paint and glued-on seed beads. Line the box with a tuft of pink tulle and fill with decadent chocolates.

Love Is in the Air

■ Give new meaning to that old saying when you mail this valentine. It starts with scored and folded red cardstock embellished with running stitches of pink embroidery floss and a heart cut from embossing foil.

Flight of Fancy

■ Dozens of colorful hearts flutter on a wreath-shape card. Use paper punches to cut hearts from vellum and lightweight decorative papers. Curl the hearts by scraping them between your thumb and a butter knife just as you would with curling ribbon. Layer them on a round cardstock base and attach each with a dab of clear glue. Sign the back and include a ribbon for hanging.

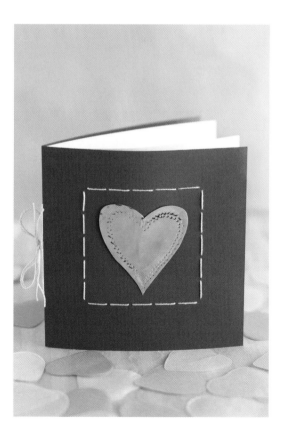

Drop Them a Line

■ The front of this card hints at the surprise inside: a miniature clothesline hung with many patterned hearts. The tiny clothespins, available at crafts stores, are too delicate to mail, so deliver this card in person.

What You'll Need...

- [ ] 7×10½-inch piece of cardstock
- [ ] scoring tool
- [ ] ruler
- [ ] bone folder
- [ ] string
- [ ] double-stick tape
- [ ] small hole punch
- [ ] heart-shape sticker
- [ ] heart punch
- [ ] decorative papers
- [ ] miniature clothespins

1 Score and fold a 7×10½-inch piece of cardstock in half using a scoring tool and a ruler. Fold against the ruler and run a bone folder up and down the back of the paper to flatten the fold. Score and fold a 5/16-inch-wide flap on both sides of the inside of the card.

2 Attach string to the inside of the card by sandwiching an end in the right flap. Close the flap with ¼-inch double-stick tape. Punch a small hole on the fold of the left flap and thread the string through. Close flap with double-stick tape.

3 Secure string at the back of the card with a heart-shape sticker.

4 Punch hearts from decorative papers and clip them onto the string with miniature clothespins.

Marital Monograms

Honor a bride and groom with a homemade gift kissed with the couple's initials or monogram.

Table Dressing

■ Add an elegant touch to fabric napkins by stenciling the couple's initials in the corners. Using fabric paint, keep color choices natural and muted for a classic look or try primary colors or pastels for a detail that's casual and fun.

Pillow Personality

■ Pump up a plain pillow with a traditional three-letter monogram, or make a bold statement with one big character. Remove the pillow stuffing and insert a flat piece of cardboard to provide support behind the fabric for stenciling and to keep paint from bleeding to the back of the pillow cover. Replace the stuffing after the paint dries.

Seat Mates

■ The inherent dressiness of monograms makes them the natural candidate for special accessories such as chair covers. Use stencils to create the pretty accents, using a color that complements, yet contrasts, the background.

"Tray" Elegant

■ Large flat accessories, such as trays, provide a perfect canvas for paint. Encircle a generous initial with a stenciled wreath motif. To use two stencils and/or different paint colors, allow the first stenciled motif to dry before starting the second.

Mark It Theirs

■ An unfinished chest of drawers becomes a focal point when painted and adorned with script initials. First paint the base color to coordinate with the newlyweds' furniture. Then use stencils and contrasting paint to add the letters and decorative accents.

Anchored in History

■ Place a bill or two under a clear glass plate and let presidential history shine through. For interest, set each person's place setting using different bills. Do a little research ahead of time to prompt a casual game of trivia.

Sweet Politics

■ To enhance the Presidents' Day theme, purchase candies wrapped like U.S. money and place them in a serving dish for all to enjoy. If desired, use the candies as prizes, one piece for each correctly answered trivia question.

Presidential Salute

Set the tone for an interesting Presidents' Day dinner discussion by inviting a few of our nation's leaders to the table.

Lucky You

Honor St. Patrick's Day with glasses etched with contemporary-style shamrocks.

Irish Etchings

■ Plain glasses go designer in minutes with this easy-to-do etching technique.

What You'll Need...

- clear or colored glasses
- ⅛×3-inch strip of adhesive label or painter's tape
- ¾-inch round labels
- etching cream
- paintbrush

1 **Wash and dry the glasses.** Avoid touching the area to be etched.

2 **Arrange the stem sticker** and four round label stickers on the glass to resemble a four-leaf clover. Press the edges down firmly.

3 **Following the manufacturer's instructions,** brush the etching cream over the stickered area in a rectangular shape with ragged edges.

4 **After the recommended etching time,** rinse off the cream with warm water. Remove the stickers and wash the glasses.

Banner Year

Celebrate family and friends' birthdays with decorations that tout the age of the person of honor. No matter what the number, you'll find plenty of party ideas to make the celebration one to remember.

Terrific Toppers

■ Circle punches and sticker numbers team up to make cute cupcake trims. From solid or subtle-patterned paper, punch out two large circles and one small circle. Sandwich a toothpick between the two large circles and use double-stick tape to adhere layers together. Center the small circle on one of the large circles. Press a number sticker in the center.

Golden Years

■ Perfect for birthday toasts, this handpainted goblet is made using just two colors of glass paint. Paint the number on the glass and underline it with a swirl; let dry. To accent the motif, dip the paintbrush handle tip in contrasting paint. Dot the left side of the numbers and swirl; let dry. Cure the paint according to the manufacturer's instructions.

Flavor Favors

■ With ice cream cones as the holders, these party favors are as clever as they are delicious! Slide a funnel-style cone into the bottom of a clear-plastic triangular frosting piping bag. Fill the cone with candies, such as gumdrops or marshmallow treats. Tie the bag with ribbon. Paper circles and stickers embellish the sweet presentation.

sweet 16

sweet 16

Sport a Look

■ Embroidered adhesive numbers add a sporty touch to party invites and thank-yous made from cardstock and decorative paper. Cut a small rectangle to back the numbers, allowing the numbers to extend beyond the edges. Use a glue stick to fasten the layers together. Tie a jute bow around the card fold.

Fit to Be Tied

■ Wood alphabet letters, blanketed with pretty papers, mark the chair of the birthday boy or girl. For years that have several letters, wood numbers can take their place. To paper the letters, trace the wrong side of the letter onto the paper back with pencil. Cut out the letter. Use decoupage medium to adhere the paper to the wood; let dry. Hot-glue a cord along the top edge of each letter, allowing long tails for tying onto the chair.

Happy 63rd Birthday! Happy 63rd Birthday! Happy 63rd Birthday!

Best Wishes Mat

Ordinary scrapbook papers make incredibly thoughtful party place mats. Simply print out a repeating birthday wish on paper to make a border mat height. Trim the top using decorative-edge scissors. Using the photo for inspiration, adhere the layers together with double-stick tape.

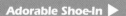

Adorable Shoe-In ▶

From baby showers to birthdays, these cute favors hold tiny treasures. Simply tuck a clean votive candleholder into a new baby shoe, slipper, or sock and you're good to go.

Easy Does It
Do Me A Favor

◀ **Open Communication**

Place your gift in a votive holder, top with a paper muffin liner, and tie with a colorful string. These little containers are just the right size for holding candy, movie tickets, lip balm, jewelry, or any tiny treasure.

▼ Clever Caps

Turn aerosol caps into pretty party favors. Cover with printed paper and tie with ribbon. For edging, fold 1-inch paper squares in half twice, tape into a chain, and hot-glue along the edge.

▲ In the Cards

Library book pockets make fashionable holders for gift card favors. Punch a pair of holes on the back and thread with a snippet of ribbon. To decorate the front, punch out a shape and back with contrasting paper glued into place. Add sparkle with a press-on gem.

◄ Rose Bowl Float

Present each guest with a beautiful bloom displayed in glass. Float flowerheads in stemless wineglasses, using warm water to help petals open fully. If desired, accompany each with a bottle of wine wrapped in decorative paper.

WELCOME SPRING

Rejuvenate your home with beautiful blooms, vibrant colors, and clever concepts that are as fresh as the season itself.

Blooming
Beauties

*Celebrate spring with creative containers
filled with lush, sweetly fragrant flowers.*

Bright
Basket

■ A vibrant display of
purple hyacinths and bright
primroses in a French
wire basket is the perfect
addition to any outdoor
setting. To make a blooming
basket, line it with irregular
pieces of sheet moss (some
types require misting with
water to soften them).
Remove plants from pots,
position them on the moss,
and add potting soil around
each plant.

Don't Be Chicken

■ Farm auctions and flea markets are full of planters-in-waiting. Rusty pieces, such as chicken feeders, prove that antiques deserve a second chance.

Light the Way

■ Paper lanterns from a set of party lights make festive vases. Insert stems into florist vials and tuck the vials into the top of the lantern. Display them on tables or use ribbon to hang lanterns on a stair rail or window frame. Carnations in unusual colors arranged in tight nosegays look surprisingly chic.

Whirling Wonders

Nothing puts a smile on faces like old-fashioned pinwheels spinning in the warm spring air. Capture the charm of these beloved toys by incorporating them into your springtime decor.

Flower Power

Attached to long dowels and embellished with gentle leaf shapes, these pinwheels add a whimsical touch to flower boxes. If desired, cut from water-resistant foam so they can weather the outdoors.

What You'll Need...

- [ ] scissors
- [ ] scrapbook papers
- [ ] ruler
- [ ] pencil
- [ ] push pins
- [ ] basswood dowels
- [ ] stickers

1 Trim paper to desired pinwheel size.

2 On the wrong side of paper, use ruler and pencil to draw an X from corner to corner.

3 Cut along drawn line, cutting no closer than ½ inch at center of X.

4 Fold the points toward the center, overlapping each one. Use a push pin to tack the pinwheel to the dowel. Place a sticker in the center.

5 Cut a paper leaf and tack the shape to the dowel.

Center of Attention

■ Give the season's inaugural picnic a boost of color with this fanciful centerpiece. In the center of the pinwheels are letters that spell out "spring." Mix and match colors and patterns and plant the pinwheels in painted flowerpots filled with simple greenery for a wildflower garden.

Playful Plaques

■ Pinwheels mounted on painted square canvases make a graphic statement. For large pinwheel art, use art papers glued back to back. Create smaller pinwheel plaques from double-sided 12-inch square scrapbook paper.

Egg-stra Special

Celebrate the Easter season by perking up your space with cheerful egg decorations.

Simply Beautiful

■ Paint dyed eggs with simple white designs for a festive tabletop. Use small artists' paintbrushes and toothpicks to create the mini motifs. If you paint both sides of the eggs, let one side dry before painting the flip side.

Spring String

■ Create interest at the table with a pastel egg garland. Use a wooden skewer and ribbon to string hollowed-out eggs. Alternate colors or use every color under the rainbow.

Mini Masterpieces

■ Turn a hollowed-out egg into a petite planter by gently breaking off the top third of the shell. Dye the eggshell and let it dry. Polka-dot the outside using a pencil eraser dipped into white crafts paint. Hot-glue the shell onto a floral mirror screw embellishment to stand it upright. Plant the tiny containers with snippets of flowers.

The Place to Be

Guests will find their spots at the table with these clever identifiers. For a quick circle pattern, use a pencil to trace around a nickel on one side of the egg. Then use white crafts paint to record each guest's first initial inside the traced circle. Dip a round toothpick into white paint and dot around the line at even intervals.

It's a Hit

■ A bright piñata sets the stage for this fiesta-flavored tablescape. Turn to the centerpiece to drive the color palette for table coverings, dinnerware, serving pieces, and additional decorations.

South of the Border Fiesta

Grab your favorite authentic Mexican recipes and celebrate Cinco de Mayo in style. Dress the table with vivid color and decorative accents to make the gathering unforgettable.

Festive Flair

■ Edge serving pieces with pretty ruffles made from 1-inch squares cut from paper napkins. Using a pencil, place the eraser end in the center of the unprinted side of the napkin, twist, dip in glue, and press in place.

On the Border

■ Give paper plates instant charm with embroidery floss stitches marching around the edge. Use a paper punch to make evenly spaced holes around the edge, then refer to the stitching guide on page 154 to add blanket stitches.

Paper Petals

■ Paper flowers, crafted from sheets of bright tissue paper, add big splashes of color to Cinco de Mayo decorating.

What You'll Need...
- ☐ 6 sheets tissue paper
- ☐ scissors
- ☐ chenille stem
- ☐ paper shred

1 Layer the papers and trim to 12×18 inches or any desired flower size.

2 Accordian-fold the short side of the paper, making 1-inch folds as shown in Photo A.

3 Secure the pleats in the center using a chenille stem as shown in Photo B.

4 Gently pull apart the layers, shaping the paper into a flower as shown in Photo C.

5 Fill the center with paper shred to cover the chenille stem and add texture to the flower center as shown in Photo D.

Posies for Mom

Surprise mom on her day in May with colorful flowers and lush plants nestled into shabby-chic vases coated with a crackle finish.

Old-World Chic

■ Terra-cotta planters take on a vintage look with a simple painting technique.

What You'll Need...

- ☐ terra-cotta planter
- ☐ acrylic paint in desired colors
- ☐ paintbrush
- ☐ crackle medium, such as Modern Masters
- ☐ crackle enhancer, such as Modern Masters
- ☐ jar or plastic glass (optional)

1 Paint the lower part of the planter the desired color; let dry.

2 Paint the planter top the desired color as shown in Photo A; let dry.

3 Paint a coat of crackle medium on the planter rim following the manufacturer's instructions as shown in Photo B.

4 Wipe on the crackle enhancer according to the manufacturer's instructions as shown in Photo C. Let the enhancer dry.

5 Fill the planter with small plants or flowers. For a fresh bouquet, line the planter with a jar or plastic cup as shown in Photo D.

The Center of It All

■ Forgo the expected wall of photos and use your graduate's mug as the launching point for table centerpieces. Thrift-store books in school colors create a fun foundation while oversize paperclips help anchor loose photos so they stay put.

Honor your superstar scholar with quick touches that sing with honor. School colors and scrapbook store accents make the prep for this A+ celebration a snap.

For the Glad Grad

Instant Mat

■ Visit your local scrapbook store to purchase 12-inch square pages dedicated to local schools. Use these personalized papers for ready-made table mats on serving or gift tables. Apply the graduation year to serving pieces temporarily, using alphabet stickers.

Good to Go

■ Paper products are time-saving when serving a houseful of guests. Carry out the school theme with plates and cups to match the color scheme. Layer plates, trimming the top plate with pinking shears. Punch holes through plates and tie with ribbons. Add the grad's initial to each cup using a sticker.

Hat's Off

■ Fashioned after a graduation cap, this little keepsake can hold a gift or serve as a party favor. Paint the base and lid contrasting colors, glue ribbon around lid edge, and adhere a stitched initial. Poke a hole in the lid center and thread with a pair of tassels, knotted on the inside to secure.

Confirmation Day

Whether it's confirmation or another special faith journey day, these projects make keepsake gifts.

So Charming

■ Available in scrapbook stores, these word-wise charms send a special message to the confirmand. Connect them to a swivel clasp attached to ribbon to make a bookmark.

Say It with Meaning

■ From the Bible passage to the color scheme, this plaque can be personalized for the recipient.

What You'll Need...

☐ 8-inch square wood plaque
☐ wood stain
☐ clear topcoat
☐ 2 coordinating scrapbook papers
☐ computer and printer
☐ 1-inch square punch
☐ decoupage medium
☐ hammer
☐ upholstery tacks

1 Stain the wood plaque as desired; let dry.

2 Topcoat stained plaque; let dry.

3 Print the desired message to fit a 3¼-inch square; print on paper and cut out.

4 Punch out forty 1-inch squares from decorative paper.

5 Adhere passage cutout to plaque center using decoupage medium. Adhere squares to plaque, leaving ⅛-inch borders around pieces.

6 Hammer an upholstery tack in the center of each paper square.

As for me
and my house
We shall serve
the Lord.

- Joshua 24:15

Photo Finish ▶

Give an everlasting bouquet with paper flowers. The stems are painted wooden dowels. A mini clothespin glued on the back of the dowel holds a photo in place. Create blooms from colored paper by using a flower punch. Accent each flower center with a scrapbooking gem.

Easy Does It
May Day Magic

◀ **The Can Can**

Recycled cans make charming little candy containers. Attach paper with glue and embellish with irresistible ribbons. Bend chenille stems to make handles; tape to cans. Top off with a handful of candy.

▼ **Bubble Bottles**

Dress up bubble bottles for kids using sticker labels and a snippet of ribbon tied around the lid. Write "Happy May Day!" on each label before adhering it to the bottle. Tuck a blower under each ribbon.

◄ Petal Power

Petal Power

Pretty a paper or plastic cup with petals. Use the pattern on page 154 to cut the collar from decorative paper. Trim as shown on the pattern and glue in place. Identify recipients by writing their names on paper cut into leaf shapes.

Just Say Aah

Invite Mom to relax in the luxury of bath salts this May Day. Use sticker label paper and spice jars to give bath notions a personalized touch. For others on your list, use initials to label the bottles.

▲ **Happy Planting**

A wire photo holder works wonders for holding an assortment of seeds for the gardener in your life. Tie a ribbon bow at the bottom and this May Day gift is presentable.

Red, White, and Blueberry Shortcake
recipe, page 89

SAVOR *the* SEASONS

Whether you're planning dinner for your sweetie on Valentine's Day, a springtime brunch, a posh picnic outing, or a feed-a-crowd barbecue, make it a memorable occasion with delicious food.

To My Valentine

Surprise your honey on Valentine's Day with a dinner that's sure to be a hit. When the meal's ready, uncork a great bottle of wine, light the candles, and let the romance begin.

Easy Mixed Grill

Marinated steak, sausage, and shrimp get a special little Valentine's Day touch when arranged facing each other to form hearts.

- 2 3- to 4-ounce beef tenderloin steaks (cut ¾ inch thick)
- 1 sweet Italian sausage link, cut into 1½- to 2-inch slices
- 4 jumbo shrimp, peeled and deveined
- 4 6-inch wooden skewers
- ¼ cup fresh lime juice or lemon juice
- 2 cloves garlic, minced
- 2 tablespoons olive oil
- 2 tablespoons chopped fresh cilantro
- ¼ teaspoon salt
- ⅛ teaspoon ground black pepper
- Fresh cilantro sprigs
- Herbed Ketchup

Place meats and shrimp in a resealable plastic bag set in a shallow dish. Soak skewers in water for 30 minutes before grilling.

For marinade, in a small bowl stir together lime juice, garlic, olive oil, chopped cilantro, salt, and pepper. Pour into bag; seal. Marinate in refrigerator up to 2 hours, turning occasionally. Drain; discard marinade. Thread 2 shrimp onto each of 2 skewers. Thread sausage onto remaining skewers.

For charcoal grill, place sausage skewers on the rack of an uncovered grill directly over medium coals. Grill for 15 minutes or until juices run clear and no pink remains (160°F), turning frequently. Grill steaks for 8 to 10 minutes for medium-rare, turning once. Grill shrimp skewers for 2 to 3 minutes per side or until shrimp are opaque.

Place steaks on a serving platter. Add cilantro sprigs. Remove shrimp from the skewers; place on top of each steak, forming a heart shape. Add sausage kabob. Serve with Herbed Ketchup. Makes 2 servings.

HERBED KETCHUP: In a food processor combine ⅓ cup olive oil; 2 tablespoons lime juice; ½ cup packed fresh parsley leaves; ½ cup packed fresh basil leaves; ½ cup packed fresh cilantro leaves; 2 cloves garlic, quartered; ¼ teaspoon salt; and ¼ teaspoon ground black pepper. Cover; process until nearly smooth. Cover and chill. Use within 2 days. Makes 8 (1-tablespoon) servings.

Salmon "Martini" Starter

Salmon "Martini" Starter

The curly green in this recipe is frisée. Any green, such as escarole or curly endive, can be substituted.

Nonstick cooking spray
1 4-ounce salmon fillet, ¾ to
    1 inch thick
½ of a medium avocado, seeded,
    peeled, and sliced
¼ of a small cucumber, halved,
    seeded, and cut into spears
½ cup grape or cherry tomatoes,
    halved
½ cup frisée, escarole, or
    lettuce leaves
2 tablespoons fresh lemon juice
2 teaspoons olive oil
   Ground black pepper

Preheat oven to 425°F. Lightly coat a shallow baking pan with cooking spray.

Place salmon, skin side down, in baking pan; sprinkle with *salt* and *ground black pepper.* Bake for 10 to 12 minutes or until fish flakes easily when tested with fork. Remove from oven; cool in pan for 10 minutes. Remove skin from salmon; discard. Break salmon into large chunks. Using a metal spatula, transfer salmon to a plate. Chill salmon for 30 minutes.

In martini glasses or small bowls arrange salmon, avocado, cucumber, tomatoes, and frisée. Combine lemon juice and olive oil; drizzle over salmon mixture. Season to taste with pepper. Cover and chill until serving time. Makes 2 servings.

Inside-Out BLTs

Inside-Out BLTs

Plum tomato halves brim with a savory bacon, lettuce, and cheese filling.

3 slices bacon, crisp-cooked,
    drained, and crumbled
⅓ cup chopped romaine lettuce
⅓ cup coarse soft bread crumbs
2 tablespoons grated Parmesan
    cheese
2 teaspoons olive oil
2 medium plum tomatoes
⅛ teaspoon ground black pepper
2 teaspoons mayonnaise
   Cherry tomatoes, halved
   (optional)

Preheat oven to 400°F. In a medium bowl combine bacon, lettuce, crumbs, cheese, and olive oil; mix well. Set aside.

Halve plum tomatoes lengthwise. Scoop out insides, leaving ¼- to ½-inch shells. Sprinkle inside of each tomato shell with pepper. Brush with some of the mayonnaise. Mound bacon mixture in tomato shells; transfer to a baking pan.

Bake stuffed tomatoes, uncovered, for 10 to 12 minutes or until tomatoes start to soften. If desired, serve with cherry tomatoes. Makes 2 servings (2 halves each).

*Sweet-and-Fiery
Polenta Fries*

Sweet-and-Fiery Polenta Fries

Cut fries from ready-made polenta and sprinkle with sugar for sweet, and chili powder and cayenne pepper for heat.

- 1 teaspoon sugar
- ¼ teaspoon salt
- ¼ teaspoon ground cumin
- ¼ teaspoon chili powder
  Dash cayenne pepper
- ½ of a 16-ounce tube refrigerated cooked polenta (cut crosswise)
- 2 tablespoons all-purpose flour
- ¼ cup canola oil
- 2 tablespoons finely chopped red sweet pepper
- 1 tablespoon chopped fresh basil or fresh Italian parsley

In a large bowl combine sugar, salt, cumin, chili powder, and cayenne pepper; set aside.

Cut polenta lengthwise in 6 thin slices; cut each slice lengthwise into 4 strips. In medium bowl toss polenta strips with flour to coat.

In a large skillet heat oil over medium-high heat. Shake excess flour off polenta strips; add polenta strips to hot oil. Cook strips for 7 to 8 minutes or until golden, turning occasionally. Drain on paper towels. Place fries in bowl with sugar mixture; toss to coat. Place on platter; sprinkle with sweet pepper and basil. Serve immediately or keep warm on baking sheet in a 325°F oven for 20 minutes. Makes 2 to 4 servings.

NOTE: To reheat leftovers, place fries in a single layer on a foil-lined baking sheet. Bake, uncovered, in a 350°F oven for 8 to 10 minutes or until hot.

Red Velvet Mini Cakes

Red Velvet Mini Cakes

Food coloring gives the rich chocolate batter a lovely red hue—how perfect for Valentine's Day.

- 3 eggs
- ¾ cup butter
- 3 cups all-purpose flour
- 2 teaspoons unsweetened cocoa powder
- 2¼ cups sugar
- 1½ teaspoons vanilla
- 1 1-ounce bottle red food coloring (2 tablespoons)
- 1½ cups buttermilk
- 1½ teaspoons baking soda
- 1½ teaspoons vinegar
  Small heart-shape chocolate cookies (optional)
  Powdered sugar (optional)

Allow eggs and butter to stand at room temperature for 30 minutes. Line twenty-eight 2½-inch cupcake pans with paper liners; set aside.

Preheat oven to 350°F. Combine flour, cocoa powder, and ¾ teaspoon *salt*; set aside. In a large mixing bowl beat butter on medium-high speed for 30 seconds. Add sugar and vanilla; beat until combined. Add eggs, one at a time, beating on medium speed. Beat in food coloring.

Alternately add flour mixture and buttermilk to egg mixture; beat after each addition just until combined. Combine baking soda and vinegar. Add to batter and beat until combined. Spoon batter into prepared pans, filling each about two-thirds full. Bake for 15 to 17 minutes or until a toothpick inserted in centers comes out clean. Cool in pan on wire rack for 5 minutes. Remove from pans. Cool completely. If desired, top with cookies and dust with powdered sugar. Makes 28 mini cakes.

Spring Brunch

Host a fabulous brunch filled with seasonal flavors and make-ahead recipes. Perfect for Mother's Day, this menu also suits baby or bridal showers or a special Sunday morning brunch.

Overnight Three-Grain Waffles

What could be more delicious than light and fluffy waffles offered with an array of luscious toppers. You'll appreciate that they can be mixed together the night before and baked in the morning.

1¼ cups all-purpose flour
1 cup yellow cornmeal
½ cup oat bran
3 tablespoons sugar
1 package active dry yeast
½ teaspoon salt
2 cups milk
2 eggs
⅓ cup cooking oil
½ cup fresh raspberries
    Assorted toppers (maple syrup, whipped cream, fresh raspberries, citrus slices, dried apricots, and/or whole pecans)

In large mixing bowl combine flour, cornmeal, bran, sugar, yeast, and salt. Add milk, eggs, and oil; beat with a rotary beater or an electric mixer for 1 minute on medium speed until thoroughly combined. Cover loosely and let stand for 1 hour at room temperature or for 2 to 24 hours in the refrigerator until mixture is bubbly and slightly thickened.

Preheat a lightly greased waffle baker (use a regular or Belgian waffle baker). Stir the ½ cup raspberries into the batter. Pour ⅔ to 1 cup batter onto grids of waffle baker (check manufacturer's directions for amount of batter to use). Close lid quickly; do not open during baking. Bake according to manufacturer's directions (allow about 3 to 4 minutes per waffle). When done, use a fork to lift waffle off grid.

Place waffles on a rack on a baking sheet and keep warm in a 300°F oven. Repeat with remaining batter. Serve with maple syrup, whipped cream, fresh or dried fruit, and/or whole pecans. Makes 4 (8-inch) waffles.

Overnight Three-Grain Waffles

*Asparagus Scramble
Sandwiches, Bacon-Cheddar
Cornmeal Biscuits*

Asparagus Scramble Sandwiches

Bacon-Cheddar Cornmeal
 Biscuits (recipe below)
 8 ounces fresh asparagus, trimmed
 and cut into bite-size pieces
 1 tablespoon butter
 12 eggs, lightly beaten
 ½ teaspoon salt
 ½ teaspoon cracked black pepper
 ¾ cup roasted red sweet peppers,
 chopped
 ¾ cup shredded Swiss cheese

Prepare Bacon-Cheddar Cornmeal Biscuits. Split biscuits horizontally and set aside.

Reduce oven to 350°F. In a large skillet cook asparagus in hot butter over medium heat about 6 minutes or until crisp-tender. Remove from skillet; set aside.

Add eggs, salt, and black pepper to skillet. Using a spatula, lift and fold cooked egg, letting uncooked egg run underneath. Cook for 4 minutes or until almost set; stir in red pepper and asparagus. Remove from heat.

Arrange bottoms of biscuits in a 15×10×1-inch baking pan; divide egg mixture and cheese among biscuit bottoms. Add biscuit tops. Bake, uncovered, for 5 to 8 minutes or until heated through and cheese is melted. Makes 8 (2-biscuit) servings.

Bacon-Cheddar Cornmeal Biscuits

Dip your biscuit cutter into flour between cuts to prevent sticking.

1¾ cups all-purpose flour
 ½ cup cornmeal
 1 tablespoon baking powder
 ¼ cup butter
 ¾ cup shredded cheddar cheese
 4 slices bacon, crisp-cooked,
 drained, and crumbled

⅔ cup milk
 1 egg, lightly beaten
 2 tablespoons snipped fresh chives

Preheat oven to 425°F. In a large bowl combine flour, cornmeal, and baking powder. Using a pastry blender, cut butter into flour mixture until butter is the size of small peas. Add cheese, bacon, ⅔ cup milk, egg, and chives; stir until moistened.
Turn out onto floured surface. Knead lightly 4 to 6 strokes or just until dough holds together. Pat or roll dough to an 8-inch square that is ½ inch thick. Using a sharp knife, cut into sixteen 2-inch squares. Transfer to a lightly greased baking sheet; brush with additional milk.
Bake for 10 to 12 minutes or until golden brown. Remove biscuits; cool on wire rack. Makes 16 biscuits.

Whole-Apple Crisp

8 medium baking apples (such as
 Macintosh or Rome)
 1 cup orange juice
 1 cup rolled oats
 ½ cup packed brown sugar
 ⅓ cup slivered almonds, toasted
 1 tablespoon all-purpose flour
 ¾ teaspoon ground cinnamon
 ¼ teaspoon ground nutmeg
 ⅓ cup butter, melted
 ⅓ cup honey
 1 6- to 7-ounce carton Greek-style
 yogurt or other creamy-style
 yogurt

Preheat oven to 350°F. Remove ½-inch slice from tops of apples. With a melon baller remove core, stopping about ½ inch from bottom of apple. Arrange prepared apples in a 3-quart rectangular baking dish. Brush with 1 tablespoon of the orange juice. (If necessary, remove a thin slice from bottoms of apples so they sit flat in baking dish; brush with some orange juice.)

Whole-Apple Crisp

In a medium bowl combine oats, brown sugar, almonds, flour, cinnamon, and nutmeg. Add butter; combine well. Fill and top apples with oat mixture.

Pour remaining orange juice around the apples and cover with foil. Bake for 50 minutes. Remove foil; bake for 10 to 15 minutes more or until tender. Cool about 30 minutes. Transfer to a platter; drizzle with honey. Serve with yogurt. Makes 8 servings.

Strawberry-Papaya Smoothies

Strawberry-Papaya Smoothies

Choose a papaya that is partially yellow and feels slightly soft when pressed. A firm, unripe papaya will ripen within a few days at room temperature.

    1   medium papaya, peeled,
        seeded, and chopped
        (1½ cups)
    1   cup fresh strawberries
    1   cup milk
    1   cup plain yogurt
    2   tablespoons honey
    6   large ice cubes or ⅔ cup
        crushed ice
        Papaya or strawberry slices
        (optional)
        Fresh mint leaves (optional)

In a blender combine half each of the papaya, strawberries, milk, yogurt, and honey. Cover and blend until smooth. With the blender running, add half of the ice cubes, one at a time, through hole in lid, blending until slushy.

Pour mixture into 2 tall glasses. Repeat with remaining ingredients. If desired, garnish with papaya and mint. Serve immediately. Makes 4 servings.

Sweet Cheese Blintzes

A honey-sweetened creamy mascarpone filling accented with a hint of lemon makes these blintzes a rich and luscious offering for brunch. Another time, serve them for dessert.

    1   8-ounce carton mascarpone or
        cottage cheese
    1   tablespoon honey
    1   tablespoon milk
    ½   teaspoon finely shredded
        lemon peel
    ¼   teaspoon anise seeds, crushed
    ¾   cup all-purpose flour
    ½   teaspoon baking powder
    2   egg whites
    ¾   cup milk
    1   egg yolk
    2   teaspoons walnut oil or
        hazelnut oil
    1½ teaspoons granulated sugar
    ½   teaspoon vanilla
        Nonstick cooking spray
    1   cup green grapes, sliced
        Powdered sugar

For filling, in a small mixing bowl beat mascarpone cheese, honey, 1 tablespoon milk, lemon peel, and anise seeds with an electric mixer on medium speed until combined. Cover and set aside.

For blintzes, in a small bowl stir together flour and baking powder; set aside.

In another small mixing bowl beat egg whites with clean beaters of an electric mixer on medium speed until soft peaks form (tips curl).

In a large mixing bowl beat together ¾ cup milk, egg yolk, walnut oil, granulated sugar, and vanilla with an electric mixer on medium speed until well combined. Add flour mixture to milk mixture and beat just until mixture is smooth. Fold in beaten egg white (texture should be similar to a milk shake).

Coat a nonstick griddle or skillet with nonstick cooking spray. Heat over medium heat for 1 to 2 minutes. To make each blintz, pour about 2 tablespoons batter onto hot griddle. Quickly spread batter to a 4- to 5-inch circle. Cook blintz pancake about 30 seconds or until light brown. Gently turn with a spatula; cook second side for 15 seconds. Invert blintz onto a plate lined with paper towels. Repeat with remaining batter to make 10 to 12 blintzes. (You may cook up to 3 or 4 blintzes at a time in a large skillet.) Place a dry paper towel between each layer of blintzes. Cover and keep warm.

To serve, spoon 1 slightly rounded tablespoon of the mascarpone mixture across each pancake just below center. Fold bottom of pancake over filling. Fold in sides; roll up. Arrange blintzes, seam sides down, in a serving bowl or on individual dessert plates. Top with grapes. Sprinkle with powdered sugar. Serve warm or at room temperature. Makes 10 to 12 servings.

Tuscan-Style Picnic

Celebrate a summer anniversary, birthday, or get-together with friends, basking in the sun and feasting alfresco style on another culture's tasty dishes.

Chateau Chicken Sandwiches and Savoy Cabbage and Fennel Slaw recipes, pages 76–77

Marinated Shrimp
and Artichokes
recipe, page 76

Chateau Chicken Sandwiches

Grilled chicken always adds flavor to a picnic sandwich. Pounding the chicken helps it cook faster. Pictured on page 74.

½ cup bottled chili sauce
¼ cup apple jelly or hot pepper jelly
2 tablespoons vinegar
2 teaspoons Dijon mustard
1 teaspoon Worcestershire sauce
¼ teaspoon chili powder
1½ pounds skinless, boneless chicken breast halves
Olive oil or cooking oil
Salt and ground black pepper
8 French-style sourdough rolls or hoagie buns, halved lengthwise and toasted
8 slices mozzarella, provolone, Swiss, white cheddar, or Monterey Jack cheese
16 cooked bacon slices and/or 6 ounces thinly sliced cooked ham or prosciutto
Thinly sliced tomato

For sauce, in a small saucepan heat and stir chili sauce and jelly over medium heat until jelly melts. Stir in vinegar, mustard, Worcestershire sauce, and chili powder; remove from heat and set aside.

Lightly pound chicken breast halves between 2 pieces of plastic wrap to about ¼-inch thickness. Brush both sides of chicken with oil; sprinkle with salt and pepper. Grill or broil as directed, then cut chicken into bite-size strips.

To grill, place chicken on rack of an uncovered grill. Grill directly over medium coals for 6 to 8 minutes or until no pink remains, turning once.

To broil, arrange the chicken on the unheated rack of a broiler pan. Broil 4 to 5 inches from heat for 6 to 8 minutes or until no pink remains, turning once.

To assemble, lightly spread the toasted roll halves with the warm sauce. Add chicken, cheese slice, bacon, and tomato slices. Top with roll tops. Wrap each sandwich in foil. If desired, chill in the refrigerator for up to 24 hours. Tote wrapped sandwiches and any remaining sauce in an insulated cooler with ice packs. **Serve chilled** or, if desired, place wrapped sandwiches on a grill rack over medium heat until heated through, turning occasionally. Serve with remaining sauce. Makes 8 servings.

Marinated Shrimp and Artichokes

Buy already peeled and cooked shrimp for this refreshing recipe. Juicy tomatoes and fresh basil add the best of summer. Pictured on page 75.

2 6-ounce jars or one 12-ounce jar marinated artichoke hearts
1½ pounds cooked, peeled, and deveined shrimp
2 cups yellow or red pear-shape tomatoes and/or cherry tomatoes or 2 cups grape tomatoes, halved if large
½ cup lemon juice
¼ cup olive oil
2 tablespoons snipped fresh basil
1 tablespoon white wine vinegar
1 tablespoon finely chopped shallot or onion
1 teaspoon sugar
2 cloves garlic, minced
½ teaspoon bottled hot pepper sauce
¼ teaspoon salt
¼ teaspoon ground black pepper

In a resealable plastic bag combine undrained artichokes, shrimp, and tomatoes; set the bag into a deep bowl.

For marinade, in a screw-top jar with a tight-fitting lid combine lemon juice, olive oil, basil, vinegar, shallot, sugar, garlic, hot pepper sauce, salt, and pepper. Cover; shake well. Pour over shrimp mixture. Seal bag; turn to coat all ingredients.

Marinate shrimp mixture in the refrigerator for 4 to 12 hours, turning bag occasionally to distribute marinade. Before serving, let stand at room temperature for 15 minutes.

To serve, drain the shrimp mixture. Serve with wooden picks. Makes 8 servings.

NOTE: For a quick marinade, substitute 1 cup zesty Italian salad dressing for the lemon juice, olive oil, sugar, shallot, garlic, salt, and hot pepper sauce. Stir in ½ teaspoon dried rosemary or Italian seasoning, crushed. Continue as directed.

MAKE-AHEAD TIP: Place marinated mixture in a plastic container and chill in the refrigerator for up to 12 hours. Transport in an insulated cooler with ice packs.

Chilled Tomato Bean Soup

Serve an assortment of cheese and fruit for a tasty appetizer.

Chilled Tomato Bean Soup

Serve this herbed tomato soup in small glasses as an appetizer or first course. Use canned tomatoes and hot-style vegetable juice instead of lots of fresh tomatoes and it's almost a no-measure recipe.

- 1 28-ounce can crushed tomatoes
- 1 15-ounce can garbanzo beans (chickpeas), rinsed and drained
- 1 14½-ounce can diced tomatoes with basil, garlic, and oregano
- 1 11½-ounce can hot-style vegetable juice
- 1 cup water
- 1 7-ounce jar roasted red sweet peppers, drained and chopped
- 1 medium cucumber, seeded and coarsely chopped
- 4 green onions, thinly sliced (½ cup)
- ½ cup snipped fresh Italian parsley
- ¼ cup lemon or lime juice
- 4 cloves garlic, minced
  Whole green onions (optional)

In a large bowl combine crushed tomatoes, garbanzo beans, undrained diced tomatoes, vegetable juice, water, roasted red sweet peppers, cucumber, sliced green onions, parsley, lemon juice, and garlic. Cover; chill for 4 to 24 hours.

To serve, ladle soup into small glasses or mugs. If desired, garnish with whole green onions. Makes 10 cups (8 to 10 side-dish servings).

MAKE-AHEAD TIP: Transfer soup to a jar or plastic container with tight-fitting lid. Cover and chill up to 24 hours. Transport in an insulated cooler with ice packs.

Savoy Cabbage and Fennel Slaw

Fennel adds a hint of anise flavor to this colorful slaw. If you're in a hurry, use purchased coleslaw mix as a shortcut for slicing the savoy cabbage. Pictured on page 74.

- 1 medium fennel bulb with leafy tops
- ⅓ cup olive oil
- ⅓ cup white balsamic or white wine vinegar
- 1 tablespoon coarse-grain brown mustard or Dijon mustard
- 1 to 2 teaspoons sugar
- ½ teaspoon salt
- ¼ teaspoon ground black pepper
- 8 cups thinly sliced savoy cabbage (about 1 small head) or one 16-ounce package (8 cups) shredded cabbage with carrot (coleslaw mix)
- 1 small zucchini, cut into 2-inch matchstick-size pieces

Remove upper stalks from fennel, including feathery leaves; reserve leaves and discard stalks. Discard any wilted outer layers on fennel bulbs; cut off a thin slice from base of each bulb. Quarter each fennel bulb lengthwise; slice very thinly.* Set aside. Chop enough of the reserved fennel leaves to equal 1 tablespoon; set aside along with a few sprigs of the feathery leaves.

For vinaigrette, in a small screw-top jar with a tight-fitting lid combine the 1 tablespoon chopped fennel leaves, olive oil, vinegar, mustard, sugar, salt, and pepper. Cover; shake well. Set aside.

In a very large serving bowl combine the sliced fennel, cabbage, and zucchini. Pour vinaigrette over cabbage mixture. Toss lightly to coat. Cover and chill for 2 to 24 hours.

To serve, garnish with reserved sprigs of feathery leaves. Makes 8 side-dish servings.

MAKE-AHEAD TIP: Place salad in a plastic container; refrigerate for up to 24 hours. Transport in an insulated cooler with ice packs.

*TIP: A mandoline makes slicing the fennel simple.

Almond Brie

Almond Brie

When shopping for this recipe, look for aged Brie. The texture is softer than younger cheese.

1   8-ounce round Brie cheese with rind (about 4 inches in diameter)
3   tablespoons orange marmalade
¼   cup sliced almonds, toasted
1   medium yellow apple or ripe pear, cored and sliced into thin wedges*
    French bread slices or assorted crackers

Preheat oven to 325°F. Cut off a thin slice from the top of the Brie to remove the rind; discard. Place Brie round in a disposable foil pan. Spread with orange marmalade, leaving a ½-inch border.

Place pan on the grill rack. Grill directly over low coals. Cover and grill for 8 to 10 minutes or until Brie is softened and warmed. Place almonds around the border.

Serve with fruit and French bread slices. Makes 8 servings.

*TIP: Dip apple or pear wedges in lemon juice to prevent browning.

Crostini Appetizers

Go the convenient route on toppers, using purchased pesto and canned beans for one and your choice of purchased olives for the other.

1   8-ounce loaf baguette-style French bread
2   tablespoons olive oil
    Ground black pepper
    Basil Pesto and White Beans or Fresh Tomato and Olives
    Small fresh basil leaves (optional)
    Finely shredded Parmesan or Asiago cheese (optional)

Preheat oven to 425°F. Bias-slice bread into ½-inch-thick slices.

Lightly brush 1 side of each slice with oil. Lightly sprinkle oiled side with some black pepper. Arrange slices in single layer on ungreased baking sheet. Bake for 4 minutes. Turn slices over; bake 3 to 4 minutes more or until crisp and light brown.

For topping, prepare either the Basil Pesto and White Beans (pictured *above*) or the Fresh Tomato and Olives.

To serve the Basil Pesto and White Beans, spread pesto topping on the oiled side of toasts. Top each with a small amount of bean mixture. If desired, sprinkle with cheese.

To serve Fresh Tomato and Olives, top with tomato mixture. If desired, sprinkle with cheese and garnish with a leaf of fresh basil. Makes 8 to 10 servings.

BASIL PESTO AND WHITE BEANS: In a small bowl combine a 9-ounce container (1 cup) basil pesto, 1 finely chopped hard-cooked egg, and 1 teaspoon lemon juice or red wine vinegar. In another small bowl combine half of a 19-ounce can cannellini (white kidney) beans or half of a 15-ounce can Great Northern beans, rinsed and drained (1 cup), 1 tablespoon thinly sliced green onion or chopped shallot, 1 tablespoon olive oil, and ⅛ teaspoon crushed red pepper.

FRESH TOMATO AND OLIVES: In a small bowl combine 1 cup seeded and finely chopped tomatoes, 1 cup coarsely chopped assorted pitted ripe olives (such as Kalamata, Gaeta, Nyon, or Mission), ⅓ cup finely chopped red onion, 2 tablespoons snipped fresh cilantro or parsley, 2 tablespoons balsamic vinegar or red wine vinegar, and 1 teaspoon minced garlic.

Tangy Citrus Lemonade

Have a plethora of strawberries or blueberries right now? Perfect! Use the same method; just sub different fruit for the raspberries.

- 6 large lemons (1½ cups juice)
- 3 medium limes (⅓ cup juice)
- ¾ to 1 cup honey or 1 cup sugar
- 6 cups water
- 2 cups fresh or frozen raspberries
  Ice cubes
  Lemon and/or lime slices
  Honey or sugar (optional)

In a 2½-quart pitcher combine lemon juice, lime juice, and ¾ to 1 cup honey. Add water and raspberries. Cover and chill for 4 to 24 hours.

Just before serving, gently stir to combine. Pour into ice-filled glasses. If desired, add lemon and/or lime slices. Sweeten to taste with additional honey or sugar. Makes 8 to 10 (6- to 8-ounce) servings.

LEMONADE TEA: Add equal parts freshly brewed iced tea and Tangy Citrus Lemonade to ice-filled glasses. Sweeten to taste with additional honey or sugar.

Chocolate Mini Cheesecakes

Chocolate Mini Cheesecakes

If you're taking these to a picnic, tote them in an insulated cooler with ice packs. Serve within 2 hours of packing them in the cooler.

- 12 vanilla wafers
- 1 8-ounce package cream cheese, softened
- 1 3-ounce package cream cheese, softened
- 3 ounces bittersweet or semisweet chocolate, melted and cooled
- ⅔ cup sugar
- 2 egg yolks
- 3 tablespoons chocolate liqueur
- 1 tablespoon milk
- 1½ teaspoons vanilla
- ⅓ cup finely chopped dried cherries or dried apricots
  Small whole or sliced strawberries or chocolate shavings (optional)

Preheat oven to 350°F. Line twelve 2½-inch muffin cups with foil bake cups. Place 1 wafer in the bottom of each muffin cup. Set cups aside.

For filling, in a medium mixing bowl beat cream cheese and chocolate with an electric mixer on medium speed until combined. Beat in sugar, egg yolks, liqueur, milk, and vanilla just until combined (do not overbeat). Stir in dried cherries. Spoon filling into each prepared cup.

Bake about 20 minutes or until set. Cool in muffin pan on a wire rack for 5 minutes. (Centers may dip slightly as they cool.) Remove cheesecakes from pans. Cool on a wire rack for 1 hour. Cover and chill for 4 to 24 hours.

If desired, garnish with chocolate shavings or strawberries before serving. Makes 12 mini cheesecakes.

Firecracker Turkey Burgers recipe, page 84

Star-Spangled
BBQ Bash

Imbue your backyard with patriotic spirit and invite friends and family

outdoors to dine on an all-American menu.

Star-Studded

■ Stars stand proudly to make place settings spectacular. Cut three same-size paper stars, fold in half, and hot-glue together. Continue the look with star gems and garland.

Firecracker Turkey Burgers

Nothing beats burgers for a summer barbecue, especially ones that are spiced with tongue-tingling chipotle peppers and topped with a creamy garlic sauce. You can vary the amount of spice to please all palates. Pictured on page 82.

- ½ cup mayonnaise or salad dressing
- ¼ cup sour cream
- 2 cloves garlic, minced
- ¼ teaspoon cracked black pepper (optional)
- ½ cup fine dry bread crumbs
- ¼ cup water
- 4 cloves garlic, minced
- 1 tablespoon chili powder
- 1 or 2 canned chipotle peppers in adobo sauce, drained and chopped
- ½ teaspoon salt
- 2 pounds ground raw turkey or ground raw chicken
- 8 kaiser rolls or hamburger buns, split
- 8 tomato slices
  Avocado slices

For sauce, in a small bowl stir together mayonnaise, sour cream, 2 cloves minced garlic, and, if desired, the cracked black pepper. Cover and chill until serving time.

For burgers, in a large bowl combine bread crumbs, water, 4 cloves minced garlic, chili powder, chipotle peppers, and salt. Add ground turkey; mix well. Shape turkey mixture into eight ¾-inch-thick patties.

Grill patties on the rack of an uncovered grill directly over medium coals for 14 to 18 minutes or until done (160°F), turning once halfway through grilling.

Serve burgers on rolls with the sauce, tomato slices, and avocado slices. Makes 8 servings.

Warm Tarragon Potato Salad

Warm Tarragon Potato Salad

Put a new spin on potato salad by tossing in crunchy bok choy and peppery radishes. Fresh tarragon enlivens the flavor of this summer side.

- 20 to 24 tiny new potatoes (2 pounds)*
- ⅓ cup salad oil
- ⅓ cup vinegar
- 1 tablespoon sugar (optional)
- 2 teaspoons snipped fresh tarragon or dill or ¼ teaspoon dried tarragon, crushed
- 1 teaspoon Dijon mustard
- 2 cups chopped bok choy (stems and greens)
- 1 cup chopped red radishes
- 1 cup thinly sliced green onions
- 4 thin slices Canadian-style bacon, chopped (2 ounces)
- ¼ teaspoon freshly ground black pepper

Summer Asparagus Slaw

Summer Asparagus Slaw

Gently steamed asparagus spears merge with shredded cabbage and carrot and bits of mint and parsley. Pour on a lemon vinaigrette dressing and you have the perfect salad for an outdoor barbecue.

  1 pound asparagus
  4 cups shredded green cabbage
  1 cup shredded radicchio
  ½ cup finely shredded carrot
  ¼ cup snipped fresh mint
  ¼ cup snipped fresh parsley
  ¼ of a small red onion, thinly sliced
  2 tablespoons olive oil
  2 tablespoons balsamic vinegar
  ½ teaspoon finely shredded lemon peel
  1 tablespoon lemon juice
  1 clove garlic, minced
  ½ teaspoon sugar (optional)
  ½ teaspoon ground black pepper
    Lemon slices (optional)

Wash asparagus. Snap off and discard woody bases. In a medium saucepan bring 1 inch of water to boiling. Place asparagus in steamer basket; cover. Steam asparagus over the boiling water for 4 to 6 minutes or until crisp-tender; drain. Gently rinse with cool water.

In a large bowl combine cabbage, radicchio, carrot, mint, parsley, and red onion. Place asparagus spears in a bowl or on a platter; top with cabbage mixture.

In a screw-top jar combine oil, balsamic vinegar, lemon peel, lemon juice, garlic, sugar (if using), and pepper; cover and shake to combine. Pour over cabbage mixture. If desired, garnish with lemon slices. Makes 8 to 10 side-dish servings.

Scrub potatoes with a stiff brush. Cut potatoes in halves or quarters. Cook potatoes in a small amount of boiling, lightly salted water about 15 minutes or until tender; drain.
For dressing, in a small screw-top jar add oil, vinegar, sugar (if desired), tarragon, and mustard. Seal jar and shake to combine. Set aside.
In a large bowl combine potatoes, bok choy, radishes, green onions,

Canadian-style bacon, and pepper. Add the dressing; toss gently to coat. Serve warm. Makes 8 servings.
*NOTE: When buying potatoes to use in potato salad, it is important to select a variety that keeps its shape when cooked. Potatoes classified as waxy, such as round reds and long whites, have a moist, smooth texture and are a good choice for salads.

Smoke-Cooked
Beef Brisket

Smoke-Cooked
Beef Brisket

To keep the underside of brisket from charring, cook the meat on foil.

  6 to 8 hardwood chunks (such as mesquite or hickory wood)
  ½ cup Dry Rub (recipe, right)
  1 5-pound fresh beef brisket
     Brisket Barbecue Sauce (recipe, far right)

For at least 1 hour before smoke-cooking, soak wood chunks in enough water to cover. Drain wood chunks before using.

Sprinkle Dry Rub evenly over all sides of brisket; rub it into the meat with your fingers. Cut a sheet of foil slightly larger than the brisket. Poke several holes in the foil. Place brisket on the foil.

In a smoker arrange preheated coals, about half the drained wood chunks, and a water pan according to the manufacturer's directions. Pour hot water into pan.

Place brisket and foil on grill rack over water pan. Cover and smoke for 5 to 6 hours or until brisket is tender. Test tenderness by inserting fork into center of brisket and twisting. When fork twists easily, brisket is ready. Add additional coals, wood chunks, and water as needed to the smoke cooker. (Do not add wood chunks after the first 2 hours of smoking. Too much smoke makes meat bitter.)

Remove brisket from smoker. Cover and let stand 15 minutes. Meanwhile, heat Brisket Barbecue Sauce in a saucepan over low heat. To serve brisket, trim away crusty outer layer; serve separately. Thinly slice brisket across the grain. Serve with Brisket Barbecue Sauce. Makes 12 servings.

Dry Rub

This rub also works wonders on fish, chicken, pork, and even vegetables. You can easily double it and store it, tightly covered, up to six months.

  ½ cup paprika
  ⅓ cup ground black pepper
  ¼ cup salt

Brisket Barbecue Sauce

¼ cup chili powder
¼ cup ground cumin
¼ cup packed brown sugar
3 tablespoons granulated sugar
2 tablespoons cayenne pepper

In a small bowl stir together the paprika, ground black pepper, salt, chili powder, ground cumin, brown sugar, granulated sugar, and cayenne pepper.

Transfer rub to a small airtight container or resealable plastic bag. Store at room temperature up to 6 months. Makes about 2 cups.

Brisket Barbecue Sauce

Although this tried-and-true barbecue sauce is delicious served with beef brisket, it's also tasty brushed on grilled chicken, spooned over grilled burgers, or spread on deli-style turkey sandwiches.

1 large onion, coarsely chopped
1 tablespoon vegetable oil
1 14½-ounce can whole tomatoes with juice, cut up
1 10¾-ounce can tomato puree
⅔ cup white vinegar
¼ cup orange juice
2 tablespoons Dijon mustard
1 tablespoon granulated sugar
1 tablespoon packed brown sugar
1 tablespoon molasses
2 teaspoons salt
1 teaspoon liquid smoke

½ teaspoon paprika
½ teaspoon ground black pepper

In a large saucepan cook onion in hot oil over medium heat about 8 minutes or until golden brown, stirring frequently. Stir in remaining ingredients. Bring to boiling; reduce heat. Simmer, uncovered, for 30 to 40 minutes or until sauce thickens, stirring occasionally. Remove pan from heat; cool sauce.

Transfer sauce, half at a time, to a blender. Cover and blend until smooth. Store, tightly covered, in the refrigerator for up to 1 month. Reheat before serving or let stand at room temperature 1 to 2 hours before serving. Makes 3½ cups sauce (enough for 12 servings).

Red, White, and
Blueberry Shortcake

Red, White, and Blueberry Shortcake

½ cup dried blueberries and/or
   cranberries (optional)
2 cups all-purpose flour
⅔ cup sugar
2 teaspoons baking powder
½ teaspoon salt
½ cup cold butter, cut into 8 to
   12 pieces
¾ cup milk
2 eggs, lightly beaten
3 cups fresh strawberries, stemmed
   and quartered
1½ cups fresh blueberries
2 tablespoons sugar
1 7-ounce can pressurized
   whipped dessert topping

Preheat oven to 375°F. If using, place the dried berries in a small bowl; cover with boiling water. Let stand for 10 minutes; drain well. Meanwhile, grease and flour a 15×10×1-inch baking pan; set aside.

In a large bowl combine flour, ⅔ cup sugar, baking powder, and salt. Using a pastry blender or 2 knives, cut in butter until mixture resembles coarse crumbs. Add milk and eggs, stirring just until dry ingredients are moistened. Stir in drained dried fruit, if using. Spoon batter into pan, spreading evenly with a thin metal spatula.

Bake for 18 to 20 minutes or until golden. Cool on a wire rack. In a medium bowl combine strawberries and blueberries. Sprinkle with 2 tablespoons sugar. Toss gently. Cover; let stand up to 1 hour.

Using a 3-inch star-shape cutter, cut shapes from cake. To serve, place a single shortcake star in a small shallow bowl or serving plate, spoon berry mixture over the shortcake, and top the berries with a squirt of whipped topping. Makes 16 to 18 servings (1 shortcake plus ¼ cup fresh berries).

Star Sugar Cookies

Star Sugar Cookies

If you like cakelike cookies, roll the dough to ¼-inch thickness and increase the baking time to 8 to 9 minutes. Because you double the thickness, you'll get half as many cookies.

1 cup butter, softened
1 cup sugar
1½ teaspoons baking powder
½ teaspoon salt
¼ teaspoon ground nutmeg
1 egg
2 tablespoons milk
1 teaspoon vanilla
3 cups all-purpose flour
   Granulated sugar, red- and blue-
   color sugar, or sprinkles

In a large bowl beat butter with electric mixer on medium to high speed for 30 seconds. Add sugar, baking powder, salt, and nutmeg. Beat until combined, scraping bowl occasionally. Beat in egg, milk, and vanilla until combined. Beat in as much flour as you can with the mixer. Stir in any remaining flour. Divide dough in half. Wrap each dough portion in clear plastic wrap and chill about 1 hour or until easy to handle.

Preheat oven to 375°F. On a lightly floured surface, roll 1 portion of dough to a ⅛-inch thickness. Keep remaining dough chilled until ready to roll. With a 1½-, 2-, 3-, or 3½-inch star-shape cookie cutter, cut dough. Place cutouts 1 inch apart on ungreased cookie sheets. Sprinkle with sugar.

Bake for 5 to 6 minutes or until edges are light brown. Transfer cookies to wire racks; cool. Makes about 108 cookies.

Frosty Treats

For an instant summer cooldown, give your favorite store-bought ice cream or sherbet the glamorous treatment, transforming everyday flavors into dazzling desserts.

Vanilla Dream Floats

You can purchase cream soda in an amber shade or clear in color. The amber shade contrasts with the light color of the ice cream.

  1½ pints cookie dough ice cream
  2 12-ounce cans or bottles
     cream soda

Place 2 large scoops of ice cream in the bottom of each of four 8-ounce glasses. Fill each glass with cream soda. Makes 4 servings.

Ice Bucket Cherry Sundaes

Sweet cherries cooked in a citrusy sauce become the juicy topping for this luscious summertime treat. Serving this out of an ice bucket keeps the ice cream cold.

- 1 quart vanilla ice cream
  Finely shredded peel and juice from 2 oranges
- 24 ounces fresh sweet cherries, pitted (about 4 cups) or 4 cups frozen pitted dark sweet cherries
- ¼ cup sugar

Scoop ice cream into an ice bucket. Cover and freeze for 4 to 6 hours or overnight.

Meanwhile, in a large saucepan stir together orange juice, 2 teaspoons of the orange peel, cherries, and sugar over medium heat. Bring mixture to boiling; reduce heat. Simmer, uncovered, until thickened, about 15 minutes. Remove from heat; cool slightly.

To serve, spoon cherry mixture over prescooped ice cream. If desired, add remaining orange peel. Makes 8 servings.

Chocolate-Hazelnut Ice Cream Sandwiches

Keep the carefree spirit of summer going into fall with these homemade ice cream sandwiches. Easy to make, the treats can be assembled in minutes, especially if you toast the nuts ahead of time.

- 16 chocolate wafers (such as Nabisco Famous Chocolate Wafers)
- ⅓ cup chocolate hazelnut spread, (such as Nutella)
- 1 pint premium chocolate ice cream
- ⅓ cup chopped toasted hazelnuts*

Spread flat side of each wafer with hazelnut spread; set aside. Scoop 8 (3 tablespoons each) ice cream balls; keep in freezer until ready to assemble.

To assemble sandwiches, remove ice cream balls from freezer; let stand for 1 minute to soften. Place 1 ice cream ball on each of 8 hazelnut-spread wafers. Top with remaining wafers; press gently together.

Sprinkle edges with nuts. Place sandwiches on baking sheet lined with waxed paper; freeze for 3 hours or until firm.

To store, place sandwiches in resealable plastic bags and freeze for up to 2 weeks. Makes 8 ice cream sandwiches

TEST KITCHEN TIP: To toast and skin hazelnuts, preheat the oven to 350°F. Spread shelled hazelnuts on a baking sheet in a single layer. Bake for 10 to 15 minutes or until the skins crackle. Wrap up the hazelnuts in a clean kitchen towel and let them steam for 5 to 10 minutes. Rub them vigorously in the towel until the skins flake off. (Note: Try rubbing the skins outdoors for easy cleanup; the flakes can get messy.) Don't be concerned if some of the skin stays on—it adds a pleasant contrasting color and flavor.

Ice Bucket Cherry Sundaes

Chocolate-Hazelnut Ice Cream Sandwiches

Mint Ice Cream Waffle Sundaes

Store extra berry sauce in an airtight container in the refrigerator up to two weeks. Spoon the sauce on pancakes and waffles too.

4 giant waffle ice cream cones
1 pint mint or pistachio ice cream
1 12-ounce jar dark chocolate or fudge ice cream topping or ½ cup Berry Sauce
   Fresh raspberries, blackberries, and/or blueberries
   Fresh mint leaves

Place each waffle cone in a tall cup or bowl. Scoop ice cream into cones. Top with ice cream topping or Berry Sauce. Add berries to top of each sundae. Sprinkle with mint leaves. Makes 4 sundaes.
BERRY SAUCE: In a medium saucepan stir together one 12-ounce package frozen unsweetened raspberries, 1 cup fresh or frozen blackberries, 1 cup fresh or frozen blueberries, and ½ cup sugar over medium heat. Bring to boiling; reduce heat. Simmer, uncovered, until thickened, about 15 minutes. Remove from heat; cool slightly. Place berry mixture in a blender. Cover and blend until smooth. Makes 2 cups.

Tropical Treat Sandwiches

Everybody loves cool sandwiches, especially when they're refreshing sherbet treats like these. Using both kinds of sherbet creates visual treats.

1 18-ounce package refrigerated sugar cookie dough
½ cup all-purpose flour
2 teaspoons milk

4 teaspoons coarse sugar or 1 teaspoon granulated sugar
1 1.75-quart container tropical fruit or rainbow sherbet

Preheat oven to 350°F. In a mixing bowl combine cookie dough and flour; knead with hands until well combined. On a lightly floured surface, roll dough, half at a time, into a 14×10-inch rectangle. Using a fluted pastry wheel or pizza cutter, cut into 3×2-inch rectangles. Place on ungreased baking sheets. Prick with a fork. Brush with milk; sprinkle with sugar.
Bake for 6 to 7 minutes or until edges are lightly browned. Cool on cookie sheet for 1 minute. Transfer to a wire rack and cool completely.
Place a large baking sheet or 15×10×1-inch pan in the freezer. Cut carton from sherbet. Place sherbet on chilled baking sheet. Using a sharp knife, cut sherbet in half lengthwise. Cut again in 1-inch slices. Halve each slice crosswise (you should have 20 slices.) Return baking sheet with sherbet slices to freezer for 1 hour or until firm.
To assemble sandwiches, place a sherbet slice between 2 cookies, sugar-sprinkled sides out. Wrap in plastic wrap; freeze for 4 hours or until firm. Cookies may be frozen for up to 3 months.

Sherbet Fruit Pops

Chilly, wet, and refreshing, these tropical ice pops are as refreshing as a cool breeze on a hot day.

10 5-ounce paper cups
    3 peeled and chopped kiwifruits
1   tablespoon sugar
1   quart raspberry or tangerine sherbet

2 to 4 tablespoons orange juice
10 flat wooden craft sticks

Arrange cups on a baking pan. In a small bowl combine chopped kiwi and sugar; divide among cups. In a large mixing bowl use an electric mixer on low speed to beat together the sherbet and orange juice until combined. Spoon sherbet mixture over kiwi, filling cups.
Cover each cup with a square of foil. Use a table knife to make a small hole in center of each foil square. Slide a wooden craft stick through each hole and into the fruit mixture in the cup. Freeze at least 6 hours or overnight.
To serve remove foil; carefully tear away cups. Serve immediately. Makes 10 pops.

Chocolate Ice Cream Fix-Ups

Start with purchased ice cream and stir in a few goodies that your dessert eaters love. They'll never guess that you took a shortcut.

2 quarts chocolate ice cream, softened

In a large bowl combine ice cream and ingredients listed for one of the variations below. Freeze ice cream for several hours or until firm. Makes 2 quarts (32 ½-cup servings).
CHOCOLATE-MINT ICE CREAM: 1 cup broken peppermint candies and ten 1½-inch-diameter chopped chocolate-covered cream-filled mint patties.
CHOCOLATE-PEANUT BUTTER ICE CREAM: 8 chocolate-covered peanut butter cups, coarsely chopped.
CHOCOLATE-ALMOND ICE CREAM: 1 cup chopped almonds, toasted.

*Mint Ice Cream
Waffle Sundaes*

*Tropical Treat
Sandwiches*

Sherbet Fruit Pops

*Chocolate Ice Cream
Fix-Ups*

Tomato and Mint Salad ▶

Slice 1½ pounds assorted heirloom tomatoes. Arrange tomato slices on small serving plates. In a small bowl whisk together 2 tablespoons red wine vinegar; 2 tablespoons olive oil; 1 clove garlic, minced; 1 teaspoon sugar; ⅛ teaspoon sea salt; and ⅛ teaspoon ground black pepper. Drizzle over tomatoes. Sprinkle tomatoes with 8 ounces feta cheese. Sprinkle with 1 cup small fresh mint leaves. Pass additional salt and pepper. Makes 6 servings.

Easy Does It
Garden-Fresh Fix-Ups

◀ **Herbed Grilled Potatoes**

In a large covered saucepan cook 2 pounds small red, yellow, and/or purple potatoes, halved, in enough boiling salted water to cover for 6 to 8 minutes or just until potatoes are tender. Drain. In a large bowl gently toss potatoes with 1 tablespoon olive oil and ½ teaspoon each salt and black pepper. Transfer potatoes to a grill pan. Place grill pan on the grill rack directly over medium heat. Grill for 16 to 18 minutes or until potatoes are tender and brown, stirring occasionally. To serve, transfer potatoes to a serving bowl. Toss with 1 tablespoon olive oil and desired fresh herb (parsley, basil, and/or rosemary). Serve warm. Makes 4 servings.

Praline Baked Apples

Preheat oven to 350°F. In a small bowl combine ½ cup apple juice and ⅛ teaspoon ground cinnamon. Divide mixture among four 6-ounce custard cups. Using an apple corer or a sharp knife, remove cores from 4 small red baking apples. Peel a strip from the top of each apple. Place apples in custard cups. Place custard cups in a shallow baking pan. In another small bowl combine ¼ cup pecans or walnuts, coarsely chopped; ¼ cup packed brown sugar; and ⅛ teaspoon ground cinnamon. Sprinkle over apples. Bake, covered, for 30 to 40 minutes or until apples are tender. Makes 4 servings.

Chocolate-Cream-Filled ▶ Strawberries

For filling, in a large mixing bowl beat one 8-ounce package and one 3-ounce package cream cheese, softened; ½ cup powdered sugar; and ¼ teaspoon vanilla until smooth. Stir in 2 tablespoons (about ½ ounce) grated semisweet chocolate. Cut a thin slice from the stem end of each of 32 large strawberries. Stand 1 berry upright on the flattened end. Cut into 4 wedges, cutting to, but not through, the stem end. Repeat with remaining berries. Gently pull apart wedges a little and pipe filling into center of berries, being careful not to pull strawberry wedges completely apart. Serve immediately or cover and chill up to 6 hours. If desired, sprinkle berries with chocolate curls before serving. Makes 32 servings.

SALUTE SUMMER

Embrace the warm-weather season with fun do-it-yourself projects to give your home a sunshiny lift.

From Shore to Chic

*Get a boutique look at a fraction
of the cost by covering furniture and
accessories with your own treasures from the sea.*

Sea Legs

■ All-white shells transform an unfinished wood
cocktail table into this leggy, mosaic-style conversation
piece. Neatly arranged rows of shells line the outer
edge of the tabletop. On the flat apron surface, large
white shells establish the pattern and small ones fit
neatly between. Organize the shells by size before
starting to make laying out the design easier.

Shell Bell

A glass cloche brings focus to a small collection of shells. The container allows the shells to stand upright while keeping the treasures dust-free.

Clearly Beautiful

Applaud the textures and shapes of creamy white shells by showcasing them in crystal-clear urns. Group a collection of the containers with or without lids for dramatic impact.

Ocean Revisited

Canning jars take on new life when filled with sand and a collection of found-at-the-shore items. Blue jars work amazingly well, lending fresh appeal.

Fun Frame

■ Fashion a striking frame using a hot-glue gun, flat photo frame, and a pile of small seashells. Start by adhering the large shells to the frame first, then fill in with smaller ones.

Dainty Pull

■ Starfish add instant seashore appeal to furniture. Use quick-bond adhesive to cement layered starfish to cabinet pulls or wherever shell accents are desired. When using shells as pulls, tug on the original pull (not the shell) to keep shells intact.

Box of Beauty

■ The lid of a papier-mâché box is the ideal place for displaying a few prized specimens. After painting the box to complement the shells, combine favorites on the lid. Line the lid and box edges with small shells in rows. Arrange flowerlike motifs on sides and add shell feet if desired.

Reflections of the Sea

Perhaps the only thing more beautiful than a single shell is a collection of them. To balance the composition of this heavily adorned mirror and simplify the process of arranging the shells, work in layers. Arrange the largest shells on the mirror frame first, then working from largest to smallest, fit shells into the remaining spaces until the whole frame is covered.

Thanks — for all you do!

You are the very best... swim coach, ball player cast!

Love for Dad

Honor dear ol' dad this Father's Day
with a gift full of sentiment.

D Is for Dad

■ Craft a tray personalized just for him, complete with heartfelt messages from the kids.

What You'll Need...

- [ ] fine sandpaper and tack cloth (optional)
- [ ] unfinished wood tray
- [ ] large flat D to fit in tray
- [ ] acrylic paint
- [ ] paintbrush
- [ ] flat wood plugs
- [ ] wood tags
- [ ] permanent fine-line marking pen
- [ ] jute string
- [ ] wood glue
- [ ] firm clear plastic sheet and 4 clear bumper pads (optional)

1 If necessary, lightly sand any rough areas on the tray until smooth. Wipe away dust using a tack cloth.

2 Paint the D the desired color; let dry. Apply a second coat if necessary and let dry.

3 Arrange the letter, plugs, and tags on the tray as desired. Use wood glue to adhere all pieces except the tags in place.

4 Write a personal message to Dad on each wooden tag. Thread tags with short lengths of jute string. Glue tags in place.

5 To use as a serving tray, cut a piece of clear plastic to fit within frame of tray. Place a clear bumper pad in each corner of the tray and rest plastic on bumpers, gluing plastic to bumpers if desired.

Pillow Persuasion

Cute as a button and easy to make, these pillows dress the house in sunshine.

Winged Wonder

■ Felt butterflies tacked in the center add dimension to a pillow front. These fluttering beauties make wonderful housewarming gifts.

What You'll Need...
- [ ] tracing paper
- [ ] printer paper
- [ ] pencil
- [ ] temporary spray adhesive
- [ ] coordinating colors of wool felt
- [ ] scissors
- [ ] purchased pillow with zippered cover
- [ ] straight pins
- [ ] sewing needle
- [ ] matching sewing thread

1 **Trace the butterfly pattern** from page 155 onto tracing paper; transfer to printer paper. Spray adhesive on the back of the paper pattern. Place it adhesive side down on the felt and smooth to adhere; carefully cut it out. Remove the pattern and reuse it to cut butterflies from each of the felt colors, reapplying the adhesive as needed.

2 **Open the pillow cover zipper.** Arrange the felt butterflies on the pillow front; pin in place.

3 **Hand-sew the butterflies** to the pillow front with several straight stitches at the center of each body, leaving the wings free to add dimension.

Pillow Perk-Up

■ Pillows—those quick-change artists of decorating—can be customized for yourself or as gifts using ribbons to match summertime decor. Sew or use iron-on fusible webbing to adhere ribbons to a pillow cover. For dimension, knot some of the ribbons before sewing. Add a few decorative buttons for darling details.

Pastel Pillows

■ Rely on basic shapes and a palette of pretty pastels to add whimsy to summertime pillows. Paint large flower or grid designs on natural cotton canvas, then stitch it into pillow covers. Leave one edge open for turning and stuff with a pillow insert. Slip-stitch closed.

Monogrammed Pillow

■ A linen napkin takes center stage as a personalized pillow front—a perfect surprise to present to family members or friends.

What You'll Need...

- ☐ ¾ yard of yellow fabric
- ☐ measuring tape
- ☐ scissors
- ☐ sewing machine and thread
- ☐ 24-inch pillow form
- ☐ three 22-inch square white linen napkins with hemstitched borders
- ☐ dressmaker's chalk, colored or disappearing-ink fabric-marking pen
- ☐ iron

NOTE: Quantities specified are for 52/54-inch-wide fabrics. All measurements include ½-inch seam allowances unless otherwise noted. Sew with right sides together unless otherwise stated.

1 From yellow fabric, cut two 25-inch squares.

2 Sew the yellow fabric squares together, leaving a 14-inch opening along one side. Turn the pillow right side out through the opening. Insert the pillow form through the opening and hand-stitch the opening closed.

3 Using colored dressmaker's chalk or a disappearing-ink fabric-marking pen, lightly mark two rows 1½ inches apart along each side of two napkins. The outside row should be 4 inches from the finished edge of the napkin. Fold the napkins along the marked lines toward the outside of the napkin to make two rows of ¼-inch-deep tucks; press. Topstitch each fold in place.

4 Cut eight 1½x18-inch strips from the second napkin. Fold each strip in half lengthwise with right sides together and raw edges aligned. Sew along the long side and one short side of each strip, leaving one short side open; trim the corners. Turn the strips right side out through the opening; press. Zigzag-stitch the opening closed.

5 Hand-stitch the zigzag end of each tie to the back edge of each pin-tucked napkin, centering one tie between each of the tucks.

6 Use your sewing machine's embroidery capabilities or a monogramming service to add a 5-inch-tall monogram to the center of one pin-tucked panel.

7 Tie the pin-tucked napkins to each side of the yellow pillow.

Fresh from the Garden

■ Invite Mother Nature's bounty to the table as the grand centerpiece. Pile clean veggies around a hurricane shade candleholder for a glorious casual look.

Delightful Dining

■ Guests love sitting down to an inviting table decked out with kitchen linens and 'round-the-house (and garden) accessories. Plaid cushions lend comfy charm. Bold sunflowers on the table and in the yard add a pleasing burst of color.

Garden-Fresh Feast

Bring a whole new meaning to outdoor dining with these super-simple ideas.

It's Your Serve

■ Who says serving buffet style is for indoors only? Invite guests to help themselves by placing foods on nearby beautifully dressed tables.

Sunny Ties

■ Real or artificial sunflower blooms make lovely ties for tablecloth corners. Gather the cloth corner and use string to tie the flower in place.

Casual Attire

■ Topped with napkin-tied silverware, new planter saucers make creative plate chargers. Choose a simple color palette and even mix-matched items look united.

Feast Favors

■ Send guests home with paper bags filled with fresh-picked goodies. A chalkboard sign serves as a gentle reminder that the bounty is there for the picking.

Map It Out

Colorful and brimming with travel possibilities, maps (new and old) transform easily into interesting art objects.

On Display

■ Keep memories of summer vacations at hand by framing destination maps. Use simple white frames and picture mats to let the colorful maps draw all the attention. When displaying the framed pieces on a mantel or shelf, accent them with simple shapes in one color so the focus remains clear.

Location, Location, Location

■ Do you know the way to San Jose? No need to ask for directions when the headboard is an atlas. Gather up outdated maps or a collection of vintage ones and decoupage them onto a headboard, following decoupage manufacturer's directions. To manage furniture curves, use small map pieces. This technique also works well with wallpaper, sheet music, and comic pages.

Be Our Guest

When company arrives this summer, welcome them to temporary living quarters with cheery and thoughtful surprises awaiting in their room.

Help Yourself

■ Toiletry samples and snacks will help guests feel right at home. Place guest-friendly items in a basket lined with pretty fabric that coordinates with the rest of the room's furnishings.

Stylish Stitches

■ Repeating geometric motifs and easy-to-master embroidery stitches add homespun charm to purchased bed sheets and pillowcases. Use disappearing fabric marker to draw the desired design onto border areas, then stitch using alternating shades of perle cotton that coordinate with the linens. For a stem stitch diagram, see page 154.

Game Day Gathering

Take on the role of cheerleader with super-fun tailgating gear that shouts the favored team's colors.

Spirit Struck

■ Whether in the back yard or the field's parking lot, you can share your team spirit with tailgating fixin's. Bandanas, available in nearly every shade, dress up tables and chairs in a jiffy. For hard-to-find colors, head to the fabric store and purchase cotton fabric in just-right tones, then tear into bandana-size squares.

Get the Scoop

■ Snacks serve up easily in a clean bandana-lined bucket.

Candy Bar

■ Cheer on the color scheme with coordinating candies. Line metal containers with paper shred or clear plastic wrap and fill with a winning combination.

Cool Idea

■ Oil pans aren't just for vehicle use anymore! Filled with ice, this brand-new basin keeps foods cold and portable at the same time.

Wrapped and Ready

■ Bandanas do double duty as silverware holders and napkins. Group utensils and tie once to fit the casual sporty theme.

Beverage Bucket

■ Fill a large metal bucket with ice to keep refreshments cold. Play up the color combo by choosing drinks that coordinate with the scheme. You just might discover a new favorite flavor.

Clever Carriers

■ Tote unbreakable metal and paper containers and plates for ease in serving food. Mini buckets, tied with coordinating ribbons are the perfect size for nuts in the shell or wrapped candies. Paper plates, punched and laced, lend a sporty look and fit snuggly into paint roller trays to keep them from blowing in the breeze. Use double-stick tape to keep secure.

Star-Struck

■ Add interest to place settings with layered paper plates in team colors. Trim top plates by punching stars or other desired shapes around the edge. The double layers add stability, especially if not using trays beneath the plates.

Art Box ▶

Metal lunch boxes, available in crafts and scrapbooking stores, make handy containers for art supplies. Cover one side with decorative paper, leaving a narrow border around the edge. Scrapbook initials, placed in all directions, label the box with personality.

Easy Does It
School Rules

◀ **Pretty Pencil Cup**

Perk up homework space with a cheery container to hold pens and pencils. Tie a coordinating ribbon around a mesh pencil cup and tie into a bow. Accent the center with layered buttons glued in place.

▼ **Fun Files**

Alphabet stickers label file folders with distinction. Choose several font types to give each file its own personality. If space runs short, use a labelmaker to create the desired word.

School Spirit

Personalize folders with the school's initials in adhesive letters. Apply them to scrapbook paper and trim a narrow border. Back with three more coordinating papers, trimming narrow borders on each layer and adhering together using glue stick. Glue the fashionable plate to the front of a folder or notebook.

Locker Letters ▼

Dress up the inside of a locker with a first initial decked with patterned paper and sparkling gems. Start with a flat pressed-wood letter, available in crafts and scrapbooking stores. Press several adhesive-backed magnets on the back. Trace around the letter on decorative paper and cut out. Use decoupage medium to adhere the paper to the letter. Trim the center of the letter with adhesive-backed gems.

◄ Cross-Stitched Marker

Young readers will love these bookmarks personalized with trendy pins. Cut and layer two 14-inch-long ribbons. Fold over the top and secure with a pin; add a second pin below it and one near the bottom. Trim the ribbon bottoms at angles, the top layer slightly shorter. Secure the top ribbon to the bottom one by stitching large embroidery-floss cross stitches.

BOO-TIFY your HOME

As Halloween creeps up, enjoy a magical brew of food, fun, and fiendish decorations.

Pretty as a Pumpkin

Get your home ready for a festive fall by turning ordinary pumpkins into eye-catching decor with clever paint, carving, and arrangements.

Patchwork and Paint

■ Mix and match shapes cut from different-color pumpkins for a custom look. Use a template to cut identical shapes out of two pumpkins and then switch the pieces.

Check It Off

■ To create this clever cutout design, draw a checkerboard design on both a white and orange pumpkin, using the same-size squares; carve along lines. Swap out the square cutouts to create a contrasting design on both pumpkins.

Inside the Lines

■ Let the pumpkin's natural lines be the guide for painting alternating colors of stripes. Use acrylic paints on a clean pumpkin for best adhesion.

Pumpkin Hollow

■ Create same-size polka dots using an apple corer or circular drill bit. Cut the holes in a zigzag pattern around the pumpkin's center for a striking look.

Nature Play

■ Fallen leaves make wonderful patterns for this leaf-studded design. Trace around a variety of leaf shapes on the pumpkin, drawing a line to divide each side in half. Use acrylic paint to fill in the shapes.

Practical
Pileup

■ Greet guests at the
door with a pumpkin
house-number sign.
Stack small, medium,
and large Cinderella
pumpkins, removing all
stems except the one
on the small pumpkin.
Trace stenciled number
outlines using a crafts
knife. Then scrape the
pumpkin skin from
the stenciled numbers,
revealing the lighter
pumpkin flesh beneath.

Mother Nature's Work

■ An assortment of mini pumpkins and fresh fall leaves knotted on twine creates a fall window swag.

Floral
Splendor

■ Remove the tops of
Lumina pumpkins and hollow
out the insides to make fall
vases. This assortment of
cattails, leaves, seasonal
berries, and orange tulips
makes a memorable autumn
display for a sideboard or
table centerpiece. Place
water-tight containers inside
pumpkins to keep flowers
fresh and prevent the
pumpkins from getting soggy.

Not-So-Scary Skeleton

The white hue of a Lumina pumpkin works perfectly for a funny face.

Mystery Guests

■ Mysterious and a wee-bit eerie, silhouettes are a perfect backdrop for a Halloween get-together. Frame up a monstrous montage with enlarged images, people or creatures, from a clipart book.

Cast a spell over your home with shadowy figures and graphic papers that put a modern spin on old-fashioned silhouettes. Just grab the scissors and a few other supplies and watch your decor take striking and scary shape.

Fun Fright in

Scary Sconce

■ This shelf bracket-turned-sconce will shed new light on your nocturnal ways. A poster board bat supported by a dowel takes flight on the bracket. Dim the lights and let the candlelight glow the mood. The bat pattern is on page 155.

Black & White

Classic Twist

■ Who says a Halloween gathering has to have orange? Black teams with white on this table for a touch of sophistication. A pop of lime green in the center adds autumn-inspired grace.

Well Adorned

■ When you're on the hunt for ways to give your house a haunting ambience, take note of the decorative doodads in arts and crafts stores. Tied around satin ribbon, these felt chandeliers—perhaps intended as gift-bag embellishments—fit right in with the silhouette theme and table decor.

Fanning the Flame

■ Scrapbooking papers turn fireplace-match holders into bewitching party favors or hostess gifts. Use a glue stick to adhere paper, then decorate with stickers, ribbons, or strips of matching paper. Press-ons, such as the swarm of bats on the vase, are a simple way to add seasonal flair to accessories too.

Rat Race

■ There's no waiting 'til the midnight hour for these little critters to make their presence known. Scattered along a stair landing, cardstock cutouts will make your guests' skin crawl. See pages 156 and 157 for patterns.

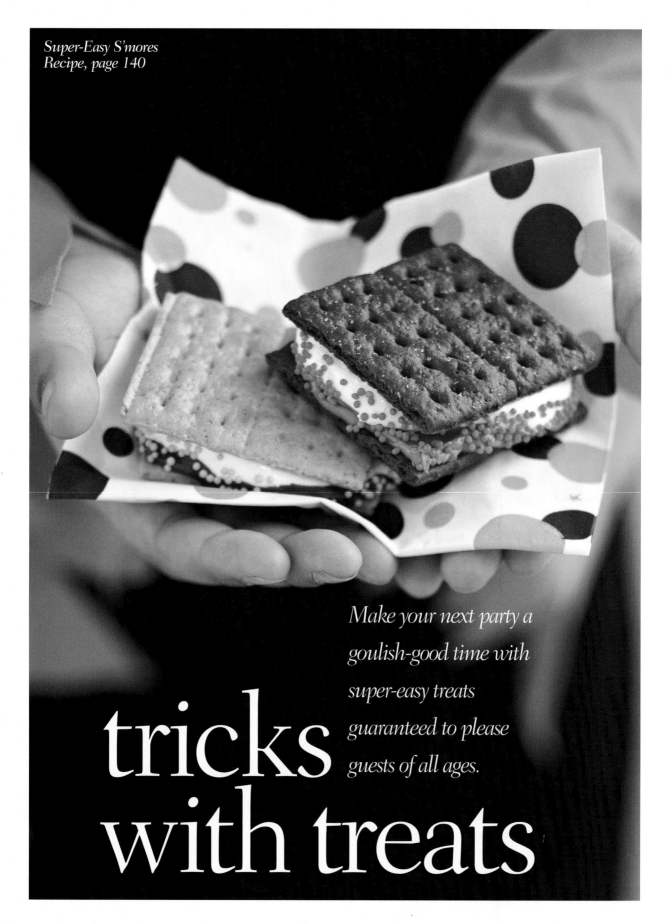

Super-Easy S'mores
Recipe, page 140

Make your next party a goulish-good time with super-easy treats guaranteed to please guests of all ages.

tricks
with treats

Mummy Dogs

Refrigerated breadstick dough makes this crowd-pleaser a cinch to make. For eyes, press capers into the dough before baking.

1 11-ounce package refrigerated
        breadsticks (12 breadsticks)
12 jumbo frankfurters
        Ketchup and mustard

Preheat oven to 375°F. Unwrap breadsticks. Stretch each breadstick to 12 inches. Wrap dough around frankfurters, letting the frankfurters show slightly through the bread. Bake for about 12 minutes or until bread is golden brown. Serve with ketchup and mustard. Makes 12 snacks.

Chicken Feed

All ghosts and goblins will love digging into this golden crunchy granola concoction. You can make it several days before the party.

- ¼ cup apple jelly
- 3 tablespoons sugar
- 2 tablespoons butter or margarine
- ½ teaspoon ground cinnamon
- 1 cup rolled oats
- ½ cup peanuts or slivered almonds
- ¼ cup shelled sunflower seeds
- ¼ cup coconut
- 1 cup candy-coated peanuts

Preheat the oven to 325°F. In a medium saucepan combine jelly, sugar, butter, and cinnamon. Cook and stir over low heat until butter is melted and sugar dissolved. Stir in the oats, peanuts, sunflower seeds, and coconut until combined.

Pour the mixture into an ungreased baking pan and spread in an even layer. Bake for 20 to 25 minutes or until lightly browned, stirring once or twice.

Transfer mixture to a large piece of foil to cool. Store in an airtight container in a cool, dry place for up to 2 weeks. Just before serving, stir in candy-coated peanuts.

Chicken Feed

Super-Easy S'mores

Ooey, gooey s'mores get their unusual name from the fact that nibblers usually ask for more. With our super-speedy version, you can have "some more" in no time flat.

- 8 chocolate or regular graham cracker squares
- 3 tablespoons chocolate-hazelnut spread
- 3 tablespoons marshmallow creme
  Orange and yellow nonpareils

Place graham cracker squares on a work surface; spread 4 squares with chocolate-hazelnut spread. Spread remaining graham cracker squares with marshmallow creme. Place graham crackers, marshmallow sides down, on top of chocolate-hazelnut spread. Place on a microwave-safe plate.

Microwave, uncovered, on 100% power (high) for 30 seconds. (If you want to heat the s'mores one or two at a time, microwave one s'more on high for 10 seconds or two s'mores for 20 seconds.) Dip edges of s'mores into orange or yellow nonpareils. Serve immediately.

PEANUT BUTTER S'MORES: Prepare as directed, except use chocolate graham cracker squares and substitute peanut butter for the chocolate-hazelnut spread.

MAKE-AHEAD TIP: Assemble s'mores up to 30 minutes before the party. Microwave just before serving.

Spiderweb Soup

Where else but on a Halloween table will you find a ghoulish makeover for everyday tomato soup. This savory bowl can be created in a snap when you follow the how-to photos, opposite.

Fill a bowl with warm tomato soup. To create the web design, prepare a mixture of 3 tablespoons sour cream and 1 tablespoon milk. Fill a plastic condiment bottle with the mixture.

Carefully squeeze several circles on the surface of warm soup. Use a wooden skewer to drag lines from the center out toward the edges to create a web design.

Super-Easy S'mores

Spiderweb Soup

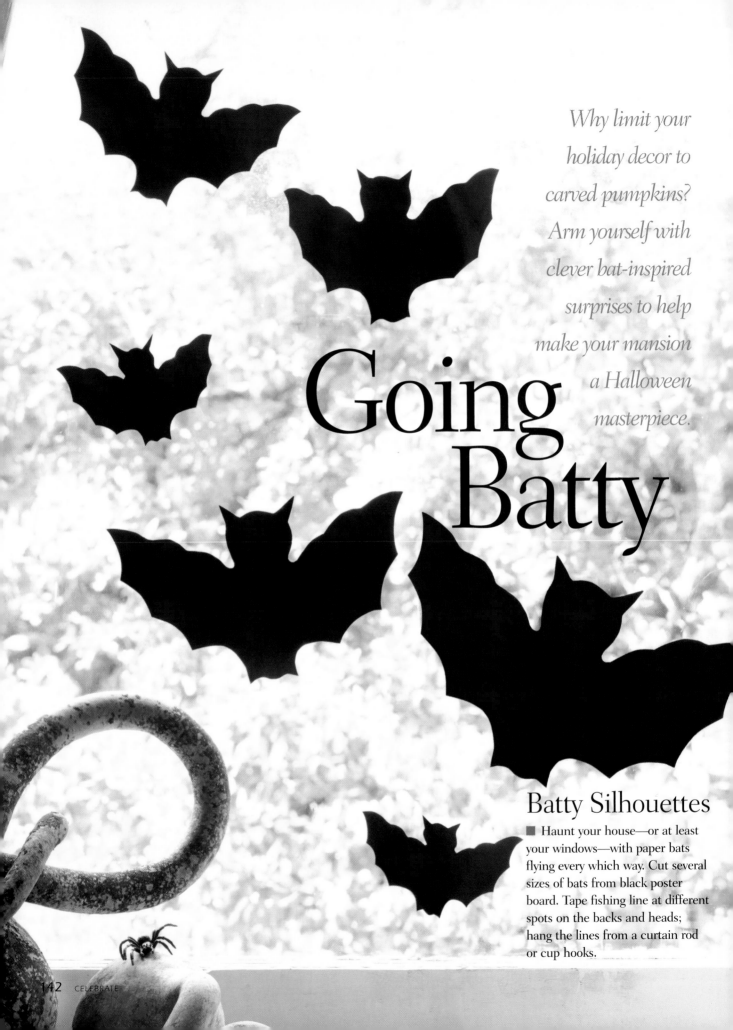

Why limit your holiday decor to carved pumpkins? Arm yourself with clever bat-inspired surprises to help make your mansion a Halloween masterpiece.

Going Batty

Batty Silhouettes

■ Haunt your house—or at least your windows—with paper bats flying every which way. Cut several sizes of bats from black poster board. Tape fishing line at different spots on the backs and heads; hang the lines from a curtain rod or cup hooks.

Perched Prowler

■ Poster board, orange glassine scraps, and chenille stems combine for three-dimensional bats. Attached to chair backs with chenille-stem feet, they give a glint of fun to the evening.

Full-Moon Frolic

■ A stick nest base holds a light globe that resembles a full moon. Add a Halloween saying written on crafts foam with permanent marker and foam bats attached to chenille stems and you're ready to welcome trick-or-treaters.

Eerie Luminarias

■ Add a warm glow to your party with black paper bats attached to inexpensive glass candleholders. Use double-stick tape to adhere the figures in place. Then cover the entire unit with orange glassine.

Show and Spell

■ Skip the carving and cast a spell by drawing bats on white pumpkins with a permanent marker. To suspend pumpkins, cut a length of thick jute and knot one end to a large washer; tie a loop in the other end. Punch holes in the top and bottom of the pumpkin and use wire to pull the twine through the holes. The washer supports the pumpkin's weight; the loop attaches to the shepherd's hook.

What You'll Need...

- [ ] tracing paper
- [ ] pencil
- [ ] scissors
- [ ] 2×3-inch piece of black crafts foam
- [ ] 12-inch square of black interfacing
- [ ] 4 black chenille stems
- [ ] hot-glue gun and glue sticks
- [ ] serrated knife
- [ ] 6-inch-diameter foam egg for body
- [ ] 3-inch diameter foam egg for head
- [ ] crafts knife
- [ ] black acrylic paint
- [ ] paintbrush
- [ ] 12-inch square of loopy chenille fabric or fantasy fur
- [ ] round wooden toothpick
- [ ] 2 red quilter's ball-head pins

Bewitching Bats

■ Every witch needs a sidekick. Some prefer cats; others like bats, as long as they're dark and scary. Round out your own guest list with furry bats swinging to and fro.

1 Trace the patterns on page 157 onto tracing paper and cut out. Cut the ears from black crafts foam and the wings from interfacing.

2 Using the wing pattern as a guide, form and cut lengths of chenille stem to outline the wings and make ribs. Glue in place and let dry. Set the ears and wings aside.

3 Using a serrated knife, cut the large egg in half lengthwise for the body. Cut a mouth notch in the small end of the small egg for the head, using the crafts knife. Also cut slits in the top of the head for the ears.

4 Paint all surfaces of the head and body halves black. Let the paint dry thoroughly.

5 Sandwich the wings between the body halves and glue in place. Let dry. Cover the body with chenille fabric and glue in place.

6 Glue the head to the body, using a toothpick to help position and hold the head in place. Glue the ears into the head slits. Insert the pins for eyes.

Fireside Fright

■ Books topped with an old seashell and a glass cloche with a blackbird inside create a haunting vignette.

Spell Bound

Sprinkle your home with tricks and treats at every turn with spirited touches that creep into the decor.

Scary Talk
▪ Flash cards propped in metal flower frogs and encased in footed apothecary jars send a spooky message.

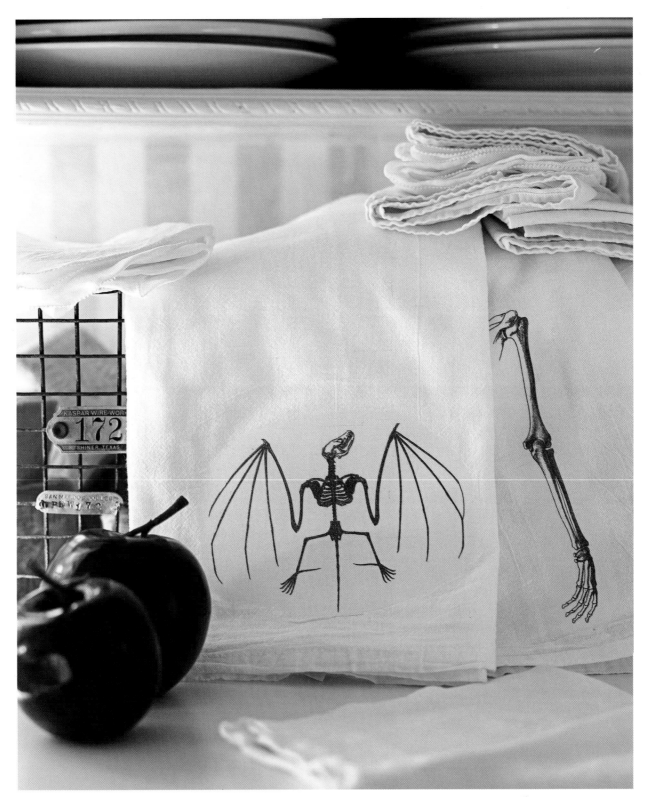

Festive Towels

■ Iron-on transfers turn plain white dish towels into Halloween hand towels. Photocopy designs from a copyright-free clipart book onto transfer paper, then iron the images onto the towels.

Bare-Bones Display

■ Bendable skeletons frolic among dishware on the open kitchen cupboards. Limiting the color scheme to black, white, and silver helps the little fellows stand out among a variety of shapes.

Reckless Abandon

■ A sideboard looks eerily deserted crisscrossed with spider webbing and a blackbird perched on top. Mismatched hardware and lamps outfitted with only wire frames for shades reflect the quirky Halloween style.

Visual Feast

■ Glass cloches make little things seem special. A fork atop a pile of plastic party favor eyeballs and a big spider are ghoulish specimens.

Ghostly Delights ▶

Tissue-paper circles embellished with punched shapes turn store-bought suckers into merry jack-o'-lanterns. An upside-down glass covered with cheesecloth and topped with a pumpkin pail makes a just-right holder for the on-a-stick treats.

Easy Does It
Not-So-Tricky Treats

◀ **Bat Bowl**

Guests can help themselves to treats with this clever serving piece. Cut a pair of bat wings (see pattern, page 158) from black crafts foam and slide them into slits cut into a plastic pumpkin bucket. Secure each wing with tape on the inside.

▼ **Ghoulish Goodies**

Transform orange and black paper drink cups into rightfully fun take-home treat containers. "Carve" the design (like that on page 158) into the side of one cup, nest a contrasting cup inside, and tie on a name tag for each guest.

Tower of Treats

Top frosted cupcakes with Halloween suckers made with candy melts and a mold. After painting the details, poke the suckers in the cupcakes baked right inside colorful latex cake cups.

Grinning-Ghoul Jars

Transform a lidded jar into a cute treat container. Cut a circle of glittered felt large enough to cover lid top and sides; glue in place. Cut off a piece from a plastic-foam ball to make a flat edge; glue to felt-covered lid. Paint ball purple; let dry. Paint pink cheeks and draw a mouth using black dimensional paint. Cut fangs, hair, ears, and a collar from crafts foam; glue in place. Glue on wiggly eyes.

Treat Tin

Instead of treat bags, dole out goody buckets. Decorate an empty, unused paint can with papers and letters. Adhere a card stock cat face (see page 158 for patterns). Spread glue on the eyes and sprinkle with mini beads for a fiendish effect.

Patterns

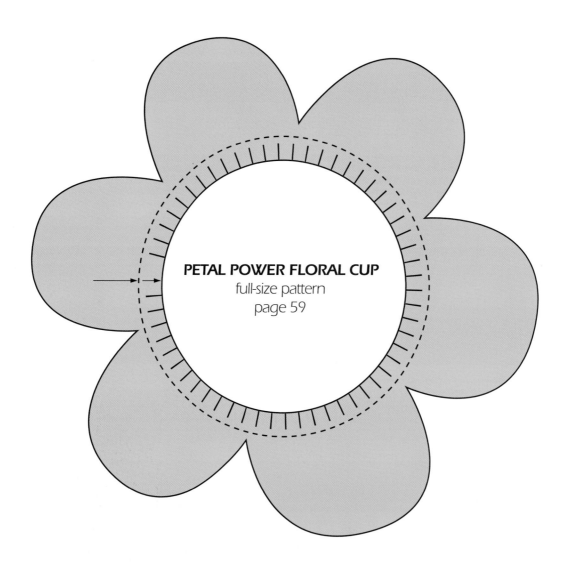

PETAL POWER FLORAL CUP
full-size pattern
page 59

STYLISH STITCHES PILLOWCASE
page 115

ON THE BORDER PLATE
page 49

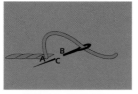

STEM STITCH

BLANKET STITCH

WINGED WONDER PILLOW
full-size pattern
pages 104-105

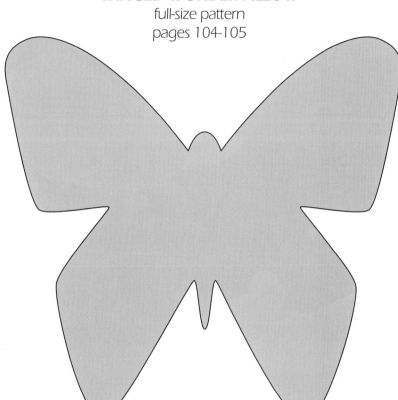

SCARY SCONCE
page 133
enlarge 200%

patterns *continued*

RAT RACE
page 137
enlarge 200%

RAT RACE
page 137
enlarge 200%

RAT RACE
page 137
enlarge 200%

RAT RACE
page 137
enlarge 200%

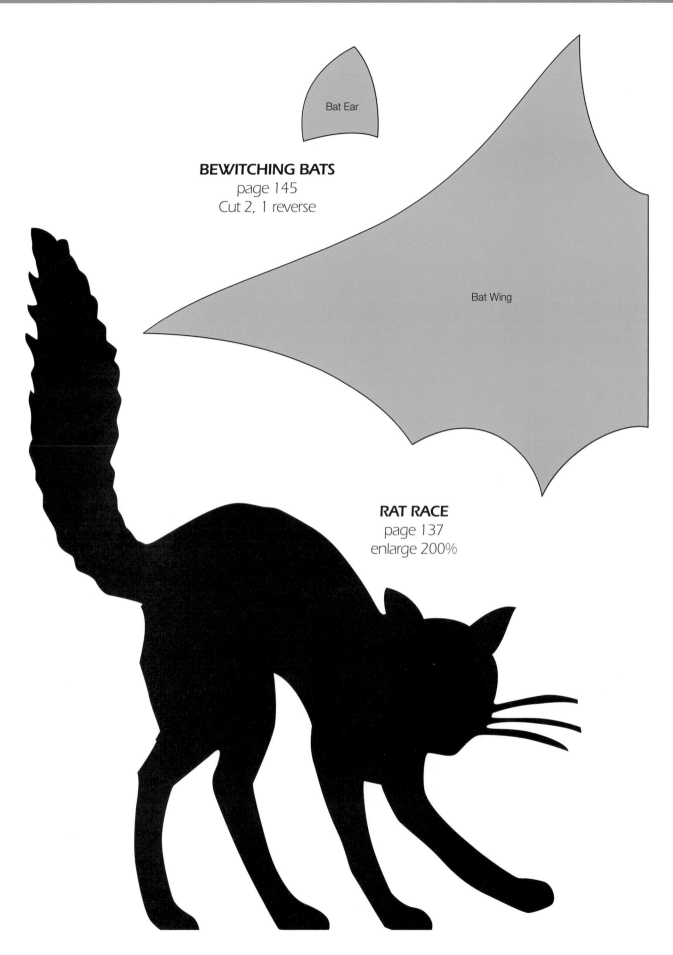

Bat Ear

BEWITCHING BATS
page 145
Cut 2, 1 reverse

Bat Wing

RAT RACE
page 137
enlarge 200%

patterns *continued*

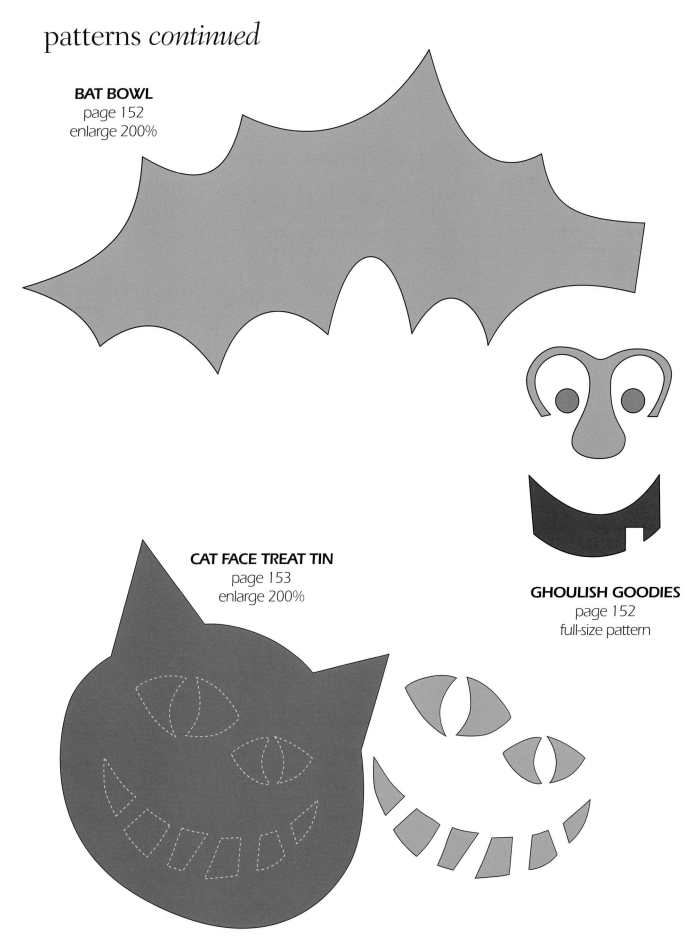

BAT BOWL
page 152
enlarge 200%

GHOULISH GOODIES
page 152
full-size pattern

CAT FACE TREAT TIN
page 153
enlarge 200%

Index

DECORATING PROJECTS & GIFTS

A–C
baskets
  flower 34–35
  guest 114
bats
  bowl 152
  candleholder 143
  chair accent 143
  flying 145
  pumpkin 144
  sconce 133
  silhouette 142
  yard decoration 143
birthday trims
  candy favor 27
  card 28
  chair marker 28
  cupcake marker 26
  place mat 29
  wineglass 26
bookmarks
  charm 56
  cross-stitched 121
boxes
  heart-shape 15
  shell 100
cards
  birthday 28
  valentine 14–17
centerpieces
  Halloween 136, 151
  photo 54–55
  veggie 108
chair cover 19
Cinco de Mayo
  flowers 50–51
  place setting 49
  serving dish 48
  tabletop 46–47
confirmation

bookmark 56
plaque 56–57

D–G
dresser 21
Easter eggs
  garland 43
  painted 42, 44–45
  place card 45
  planter 44
Father's Day
  tray 102–103
favors
  candy in cone 27
  candy cap 31
  fresh veggie 111
  library card pocket 31
  rose bowl 31
  shoe 30
  votive holder 30
flower arrangements
  chicken feeder 36
  hanging lantern 37
  wire basket 34–35
flowerpot
  crackled 52–53
flowers
  paper 50–51
  photo holder 58
football party 116–119
frame
  shell 100
glasses
  shamrock 24–25
  wine 26
graduation
  dishes 55
  favor 55
  mat 55
  photo centerpiece 54

H–K
Halloween decor

bats 142–145
displays 146–151
eyeballs under
  glass 151
pumpkins 124–131
silhouettes 132–137
skeletons 148–149
towels 148
Halloween treats and
  containers
  bat bowl 152
  cupcakes 153
  cups 152
  Dracula jars 153
  recipes 138–141
  suckers 152
  tins 153
jars
  Halloween 147,
    151, 153
  photo 10

L–N
linens, stitched 114–115
maps
  framed pictures 112
  headboard 112–113
May Day
  bath salt container 59
  bubble favor 58
  can treat holder 58
  cup treat holder 59
  flower photo holder 58
  seed display 59
monograms
  chair cover 19
  dresser 21
  napkins 18–19
  pillow 19, 107
  tray 20
Mother's Day
  flowerpots 52–53
napkins,

monogram 18

O–R
photos
  centerpiece 54
  jar 10
  pillow 11
  plate 12–13
pillows
  butterfly 104–105
  monogram 19, 107
  painted 106
  photo 11
  ribbon 104
  stitched case 115
pinwheels
  flower 38–40
  wall decor 41
place mats,
  birthday 29
place settings
  Cinco de Mayo 49
  picnic 111
  Presidents' Day 22–23
  souvenir 8
  tailgating 119
plates
  laced 118
  photo 12–13
  star punched 119
  stitched 49
Presidents' Day 22–23
pumpkins
  bat 144
  checkerboard 124–26
  garland 129
  house numbers 128
  leaf 124, 127
  polka dot 124–125,
    127
  skeleton 131
  striped 127
  vase 130, 131

index *continued*

S–V

school
  art box 120
  bookmark 121
  folders 120, 121
  locker letter 121
  pencil cup 120
shells
  box 100
  cloche display 99
  frame 100
  jar display 99
  knob 100
  mirror 101
  table 98
  urn display 99
silhouettes
  bat sconce 133
  bat 142–144
  cat and rat 137
  framed head 132
  match holder 136
  napkin 135
  placesetting 134
St. Patrick's Day
  glasses 24–25
tablecloth tie 111
tabletops
  cabin style 9
  Cinco de
    Mayo 46–49
  Halloween
    silhouette 134
  picnic 109–110
  Presidents'
    Day 22–23
tailgating 117–119
trays
  dad 102–103
  monogram 20
  photo 11
Valentine's Day
  box 15
  cards 14–17
  wreath 15

W–Z

wall decorations
  map 112
  pinwheel 41
wedding monogram
  projects 18–21

RECIPES

APPETIZERS

Almond Brie 79
Crostini Appetizers 79
Inside-Out BLTs 65
Salmon "Martini"
  Starter 65

BEVERAGES

Lemonade Tea 81
Strawberry-Papaya
  Smoothies 72
Tangy Citrus
  Lemonade 81
Vanilla Dream Floats 90

BREADS

Bacon-Cheddar
  Cornmeal Biscuits 71
Crostini Appetizers 79

BREAKFAST DISHES

Asparagus Scramble
  Sandwiches 71
Bacon-Cheddar
  Cornmeal Biscuits 71
Overnight Three-Grain
  Waffles 69
Sweet Cheese
  Blintzes 72
Whole-Apple Crisp 71

DESSERTS

Chocolate-
  Cream-Filled
  Strawberries 95
Chocolate Mini
  Cheesecakes 81

Peanut Butter
  S'mores 140
Praline Baked
  Apples 95
Red Velvet Mini
  Cakes 67
Red, White, and
  Blueberry
  Shortcake 89
Star Sugar Cookies 89
Super-Easy
  S'mores 140
Whole-Apple Crisp 71

FISH & SEAFOOD

Marinated Shrimp
  and Artichokes 76
Salmon "Martini"
  Starter 65

ICE CREAM

Chocolate-Hazelnut
  Ice Cream
  Sandwiches 91
Chocolate Ice Cream
  Fix-Ups 92
Ice Bucket Cherry
  Sundaes 91
Mint Ice Cream
  Waffle Sundaes 92
Sherbet Fruit
  Pops 92
Tropical Treat
  Sandwiches 92
Vanilla Dream
  Floats 90

MEATS & POULTRY

Chateau Chicken
  Sandwiches 76
Firecracker Turkey
  Burgers 84
Easy Mixed Grill 63
Mummy Dogs 139
Smoke-Cooked Beef
  Brisket 86

SALADS

Savoy Cabbage and
  Fennel Slaw 77
Summer Asparagus
  Slaw 85
Tomato and Mint
  Salad 94
Warm Tarragon Potato
  Salad 84

SAUCES & RUBS

Berry Sauce 92
Brisket Barbecue
  Sauce 87
Dry Rub 86
Herbed Ketchup 63

SNACKS & SPREADS

Basil Pesto and White
  Beans 79
Chicken Feed 140
Fresh Tomato and
  Olives 79

SOUPS

Chilled Tomato Bean
  Soup 77
Spiderweb Soup 140

VEGETABLES

Herbed Grilled
  Potatoes 94
Summer Asparagus
  Slaw 85
Sweet-and-Fiery Polenta
  Fries 67
Warm Tarragon Potato
  Salad 84